COOL
EATING

COOL EATING

Recipes by Louise Pickford

Photographs by Ian Wallace

CASSELL ILLUSTRATED

First published in Great Britain in 2005 by Cassell Illustrated,
a division of Octopus Publishing Group Limited
2-4 Heron Quays, London E14 4JP

A CIP catalogue record for this book is available from the British Library.

4

ISBN 1 84403 288 4
EAN 9781844032884

Recipes by Louise Pickford
Photographs by Ian Wallace

Printed in Hong Kong

CONTENTS

COOL EATING

Wouldn't it be great if we all had the time and money to shop daily? If that doesn't sound like you, but you love food and want to cook regularly then this book provides the ideal solution. Cool Eating offers a comprehensive guide on how to plan your weekly meals, shop efficiently and cost-effectively, store fresh produce safely and use those ingredients to cook creative, healthy and delicious meals.

A well-stocked store cupboard is a must; many staples such as pasta, rice and lentils are cheap, nutritious, tasty and bulk out meals. How satisfying would it be to open your fridge and find it overflowing with a wonderful array of delicious vegetables and ripe fruit, a plump chicken or bag of glistening fresh prawns?

The recipes are designed to inspire all cooks, experienced or not, to have fun in the kitchen. Recipes are colour-coded according to simplicity so you can immediately find a recipe to suit your standard and, as you become more confident, you can experiment with more involved dishes. Most recipes serve 2 (unless stated) but can easily be doubled for when friends and family drop by.

Cool Eating will enable the time-poor cook not only to organise and plan the week ahead but to ensure that a well-stocked store cupboard and fridge can mean a healthy, tasty meal at any time. There are great health benefits too – by avoiding ready meals and take-aways you will cut down on fat, salt, sugar and other additives.

Whether you are a first-time cook or a seasoned professional this book will help inspire you to cook delicious, fresh-tasting food that is cheap to buy and quick to prepare. If you follow the advice over the next few pages you will no longer come home to an empty fridge or the same old meal night after night; instead Cool Eating will expand your culinary repertoire providing you with a wide variety of delicious dishes to choose from.

PLANNING

The store cupboard
To be creative in the kitchen you need a well-stocked store cupboard – for example, dried pasta, a tin of tomatoes, a selection of spices or bag of sugar – and at times the contents of your store cupboard may be the only option for dinner. The basics are listed overleaf and a comprehensive list of bare necessities and optional extras can be found on pages 14 and 15.

Oil – extra virgin olive oil and vegetable oil are essential

Vinegar – white wine vinegar, red wine vinegar and balsamic

Canned tomatoes – chopped tomatoes are best

Canned fish – tuna in olive oil and canned anchovies are healthy and tasty

Pulses – use canned for convenience and keep a good selection, such as chickpeas and kidney beans

Pasta – a selection of types such as spaghetti, penne and fusilli

Spices – these can be collected gradually – try to add a new spice each week

Salt and pepper – always cook using sea salt and freshly ground black peppercorns for maximum flavour

Rice – keep a selection of basmati, long-grain and arborio (risotto) rice

Noodles – keep a selection including flat, egg thread, Udon, wavy

Flour – plain and self-raising are essential

Sugar – caster sugar is a must, and soft brown sugar great for extra flavour

Capers – a handy ingredient, capers add a lovely piquancy to dishes

Asian sauces – keep a selection such as soy, oyster, hoisin and Thai sweet chilli sauce – all add great flavour to dishes.

The fridge

With your cupboard well-stocked for any occasion, fresh produce needs more careful planning. Cool Eating is all about what to buy to stock your fridge – this will ensure that you have all you need for a tasty, nutritious evening meal.

Over-buying is a waste both of food and money and it's heartbreaking to find out-of-date meat or fish because good intentions don't come to fruition. Even the best-laid plans can be dashed, but I find a good compromise is to plan for two servings of fresh meat or poultry, two servings of fish or seafood with the remainder being made up of vegetable-based dishes for a week's healthy eating. Not only will this provide you with variety but also flexibility, so if the Monday night in becomes Monday night out with friends, the planned supper will keep until Tuesday.

Other items you should also keep stocked in the fridge are eggs and dairy items; these tend to keep for at least a week and some for longer (always check the 'use by date' on the label).

The freezer

Don't forget the freezer; it can be really useful to have frozen pastry sheets, frozen summer berries (when fresh are out of season) and ice cream. You can also freeze leftovers for later use.

SHOPPING

Before shopping, make a list of any essentials that need replenishing from both storecupboard and fridge. Then you can flip through the chapters in Cool Eating to inspire you for the days ahead. Buy a good cross-section of fresh produce – butter, cream, milk, eggs, cheese, two types of meat, two types of fish or seafood, chicken, a variety of fresh fruits and vegetables and a couple of fresh herbs. This quantity and variety of fresh ingredients should enable you to find something yummy to eat, whenever you cook.

One big shop a week is the maximum most of us have time for. Supermarkets now stock a massive range of good quality fresh produce. If your budget can stretch to it, treat yourself occasionally to some organic produce and see for yourself if there is a difference in taste and quality. If you are fortunate enough to live near a good butcher, greengrocer or fishmonger, make the most of them; build up a good relationship with the shop owner – it can be really beneficial and rewarding for both parties.

Shopping seasonally is important, fresh produce tastes better and will be more economical. When a fresh ingredient is cheaper it's a sure sign it is in season. So when shopping for fresh ingredients buy the best quality you can find. If possible, handle vegetables and fruit – they should feel firm, appear smooth and not wrinkled. Salads and herbs should be perky.

Supermarkets sell a wide variety of different cuts of both meat and poultry and the prices tend to be reasonable. Check the 'sell by' and 'use by' dates on the labels and only buy meat that looks fresh (it should appear vibrant not tired). Butcher shops offer individual portions which saves you having to buy pre-packaged quantities. Talk to your butcher, ask his advice on what's good or cheap this week – meat is seasonal too.

The demand for seafood is on the increase. Supermarkets are expanding their seafood departments and many offer fresh fish counters where you can choose from a wide variety of fish and shellfish. Seafood is good for you, many types of fish are high in protein, low in saturated fats and high in Omega 3 essential fatty acids and B vitamins. Ask your fishmonger what is fresh in on the day and remember fishmongers will gladly prepare fish for you (scaling, gutting and filleting). Fish should appear 'fresh', their eyes should be bright, gills red and all seafood should smell of the sea and not 'fishy'.

STORAGE

Fruit and vegetables

Store potatoes, onions, garlic, apples and bananas in a cool dark place. Store others in the fridge. Use the salad drawers for salad and herbs. Put herbs in a plastic bag (zip lock is best) with a little splash of water. Store mushrooms in a paper or cloth bag as they 'sweat' in plastic and spoil quickly. Store heavy items on the bottom and more delicate ones on top.

Meat and poultry

Remove meat and poultry form the plastic-wrapped containers, wash and dry with kitchen towel. Place on a plate and cover loosely with foil.
Always store fresh meat and poultry on the bottom shelf so that raw juices cannot drip down on to other foods.

The pictures which open each chapter show meat and poultry uncovered, and the shelves are arranged so that the foodstuffs can be seen clearly.

Always arrange your own fridge as described above.

Seafood

Seafood, like meat and poultry, can be removed from its plastic wrapping. Mussels and clams can be soaked in cold water, which helps clean out their digestive systems. Place in a large bowl, cover with water and throw in a handful of wholemeal flour or bran.

Eggs and Dairy

Dairy is fine stored as it comes. Eggs should be kept in the refrigerator but need to be returned to room temperature before use.

If you have bought fresh meat, poultry or fish and are not able to cook it before the 'use by' date, freeze it. Wrap meat, poultry and fish in foil and place in the freezer. Always thaw frozen food at room temperature until completely defrosted before cooking.

COOKING

Recipes

Because you will have plenty of fresh produce and staples to hand it'll be easy to find something appealing in the following pages. The recipes are divided into chapters determined by type of food: Chicken; Pork, Beef and Lamb; Fish and Seafood; Vegetables; Fruit; Eggs and Dairy so if you fancy chicken tonight you'll find plenty of exciting dishes to choose from.

Because this book is aimed at time-poor, less experienced cooks the recipes have been colour-coded on the thumb tabs to help you find a recipe that suits your standard of cooking. Here's how to find the perfect recipe for your dinner.

Blue is for super simple and is suitable for those who have had little or no kitchen experience.

Red is for quick and easy and requires a basic knowledge of cooking, but nothing too scary or time-consuming.

Green is for everyday recipes for those who cook often and are happy to have a go at something more complex.

That said, all the recipes in Cool Eating are easily achievable. There are dishes for all occasions, featuring cuisines from all around the world. Once you've decided what to cook, here a few simple guidelines to ensure success.

- Always read through the whole recipe

- Make sure that you have everything you need, including equipment

- Prepare everything before you begin cooking – chopping, slicing, weighing, etc.

- Preheat the oven, grill or ridged grill pan ahead of time

EQUIPMENT

Buying cooking equipment can be expensive, but these items are an investment, and you don't have buy everything at once. Here is my guide to a few basic essentials:

- Selection of three saucepans: small, medium and large

- Heavy-based frying pan

- Roasting pan

- Baking tray

- A set of scales

- 3 sharp knives: one small, one large and one serrated-edged knife

- Selection of mixing bowls ranging from ramekin size to large

- Measuring jug (plastic is fine)

- Two chopping boards (one for raw food and one for everything else)

- Sieve

- Oven thermometer

- A ridged grill pan, for healthy fast cooking

- A food processor
  This is useful not essential, but remember they are incredibly versatile and time-saving and will last you a lifetime if looked after properly.

All that is left now is to have some fun with the recipes in *Cool Eating*. Get busy in the kitchen and enjoy yourself!

THE STORE CUPBOARD

If you cook every dish in Cool Eating, your store cupboard will finally include all the items shown in the following pages, in both bare necessities and the optional extras, and you will be able to conjure up an instant meal at any time. Try to store pasta, noodles, rice, flour, sugar, oats and other dried goods in airtight containers. Check 'use by' dates regularly and buy herbs and spices in fairly small quantities as they will lose their flavour over time. Once opened, some sauces, relishes and preserves need to be stored in the fridge. Always check the labels. Don't forget to replace store cupboard staples, like canned tomatoes, anchovies and capers as you use them.

BARE NECESSITIES

Oils
Extra virgin olive oil
Vegetable oil
Sunflower oil

Canned chopped tomatoes

Sea salt
Black peppercorns

Dark soy sauce
Light soy sauce
Sweet soy sauce

Pasta
Spaghetti
Penne
Tagliatelli

Noodles
Chinese egg thread noodles

Rice
Jasmine rice
Basmati rice
Arborio (Risotto) rice
Long-grain rice

Flour
Self-raising flour
Plain flour

Sugar
Caster sugar
Icing sugar
Soft brown sugar
Demerara sugar

Bicarbonate of soda
Baking powder

Dried Herbs and Spices
Oregano
Sage
Rosemary
Thyme
Parsley
Marjoram
Coriander
Curry powder

Stock cubes
Vegetable
Fish
Chicken
Beef or lamb

Canned fish
Tuna in oil
Anchovies in brine

Vinegars
White wine vinegar
Red wine vinegar
Balsamic vinegar

Tomato purée
Tomato ketchup

OPTIONAL EXTRAS

Oils
Peanut oil
Walnut oil
Sesame oil

Mustards
Wholegrain
Dijon

Sauces
Worcestershire sauce
Oyster sauce
Thai fish sauce
Hoisin sauce
Sweet chilli sauce
Chilli bean sauce

Dried Herbs and Spices
Chinese five-spice powder
Ground cinnamon
Stick cinnamon
Vanilla pods
Ground cardamom
Ground nutmeg
Ground cloves
Whole cloves
Ground almonds
Ground ginger
Turmeric
Cumin
Coriander
Garam masala
Dried red chilli flakes
Szechuan peppercorns
Dried bay leaves
Kaffir lime leaves
Curry paste, mild and medium

Preserves and Chutneys
Mango chutney
Clear honey
Maple syrup
Lemon curd
Nuts
Pine nuts
Pecan nuts
Walnuts
Cashew nuts

Pulses
Borlotti beans
Cannellini beans
Red lentils
Puy lentils

Extra extras
Rolled oats
Couscous

Rosewater
Dried fruit
Fast-acting yeast
Sun-dried tomato paste
Olive tapenade
Anchovies in oil
Olives
Chinese rice wine
Sherry vinegar
Marsala
Mirin
Sake

CHICKEN

From your weekly shop and your basic store cupboard you can make any one of the chicken dishes shown below. The fresh ingredients that you will need are highlighted in the fridge. Some recipes will need extra ingredients or vegetables to serve which do not need to be stored in the fridge. These are shown on the shopping list. Always read through the recipe you choose to make sure that you have all the ingredients to hand.

LEMONGRASS
FRESH TARRAGON
THAI BASIL LEAVES
FRESH ROOT GINGER
GARLIC
POTATOES
ONIONS
BABY SWEETCORN
MANGETOUT
ASPARAGUS SPEARS
SPINACH
SAKE OR DRY SHERRY
DRY WHITE WINE
RICE WINE VINEGAR
TIKKA MASALA PASTE
THAI FISH SAUCE
CHINESE FIVE-SPICE POWDER
KAFFIR LIME LEAVES
DRIED RED CHILLI FLAKES
PINE NUTS
MANGO CHUTNEY
SMOOTH PEANUT BUTTER
HONEY
COCONUT MILK
COCONUT CREAM
PEANUT OIL
CHILLED OR FROZEN PUFF PASTRY
CHAPATI OR PITTA BREAD
BURGER BUNS
BAGUETTES
FAST-ACTING YEAST
JASMINE RICE
CANNED BAMBOO SHOOTS
CAPERS IN BRINE
BAMBOO SKEWERS

CLASSIC ROAST CHICKEN WITH TARRAGON

Serves: 4
Preparation time: 10 minutes
Cooking time: 1 hour

Tarragon has a natural affinity with chicken and adds a wonderful flavour to the bird as it cooks, not to mention the fabulous smells that waft from the oven. Serve the chicken with roast potatoes and a selection of your favourite vegetables.

1.5 kg (3 lb) free-range chicken
1 bunch fresh tarragon
25 g (1 oz) butter, softened
salt and pepper
4 garlic cloves, peeled but left whole
$1/2$ lemon
50 ml (2 fl oz) dry white wine
50 ml (2 fl oz) water

roast potatoes and a selection of vegetables, to serve

Preheat the oven to 220°C/425°F/Gas Mark 7. Place the chicken on a board and, using a sharp knife, score 3 deep slashes into each drumstick. Chop 2 tablespoons of the tarragon and beat into the butter with a little salt and pepper. Spread the herb butter all over the chicken, pressing down into the score marks. Put the remaining tarragon into the bird's cavity with the garlic and lemon.

Place the chicken in a roasting pan and roast for 1 hour, basting every 15 minutes with the pan juices. Remove from the oven and wrap the chicken loosely in foil. Rest for 15 minutes.

Place the roasting tin on a low heat, add the wine and simmer for 2 minutes, then add the water and simmer gently for 2–3 minutes until the gravy is thickened slightly, adding the juices that have accumulated in the cavity of the chicken.

Carve the chicken and serve with the gravy, roast potatoes and vegetables.

YAKATORI CHICKEN WITH CUCUMBER SALAD

Serves: 2 as a starter
Preparation time: 10 minutes, plus marinating
Cooking time: 15 minutes

Sake is Japanese rice wine and is often served warm. It is also used extensively in cooking and is available from good supermarkets and Asian stores. You could use dry sherry instead.

$1^1/_2$ tbsp dark soy sauce
1 tbsp sake
$^1/_2$ tbsp caster sugar
250 g (8 oz) boneless chicken thighs

Pickled cucumber salad:
2 tbsp rice wine vinegar
2 tbsp water
1 tbsp caster sugar
$^1/_2$ cucumber, deseeded and sliced
1 large red chilli, deseeded and finely chopped

bamboo skewers soaked in cold water for 30 minutes

Make the pickled cucumber salad: put the vinegar, water and sugar into a small saucepan and heat gently to dissolve the sugar. Simmer for 3 minutes, remove from the heat and leave to cool. Pour the mixture over the cucumber and chilli and set aside for 30 minutes.

Stir the soy sauce, sake and sugar together until the sugar is dissolved.

Cut the chicken into bite-sized pieces, place in a bowl and pour over the soy mixture. Leave to marinate for 10 minutes and then thread on to four bamboo skewers, reserving the marinade.

Preheat the grill to high and grill the chicken skewers for 6 minutes each side. Pour over the marinade and cook for a further 1 minute each side until well-glazed. Serve with the cucumber salad.

CHICKEN TIKKA AND RAITA WRAP

Serves: 2
Preparation time: 10 minutes
Cooking time: 10 minutes

Chapati are available vacuum-packed from the bread section of most larger supermarkets. Alternatively use pitta bread.

2 skinless chicken thigh fillets
1 tbsp tikka masala paste
$1/2$ tbsp mango chutney (sauce only)
salt and pepper
2 ready-made chapati
25 g (1 oz) shredded iceberg lettuce
1 tomato, diced
1 spring onion, finely sliced

Raita:
75 g (3 oz) Greek-style natural yogurt
1 small garlic clove, crushed
1 tablespoon chopped fresh mint

lemon wedges, to squeeze

Place the chicken in a bowl with the tikka masala paste, mango chutney and a little salt and pepper and stir well to coat the meat evenly. Preheat the grill to high and cook the chicken for 4–5 minutes each side until charred and cooked through. Rest for 5 minutes, then cut into thick slices.

Make the raita: combine the ingredients in a bowl and season to taste.

Lay the chapati flat and arrange some lettuce down the middle, top with the tomato, spring onion, chicken and a spoonful of the raita. Roll up and serve at once.

CHICKEN, MUSHROOM AND ROSEMARY PIZZA

Serves: 2
Preparation time: 20 minutes
Cooking time: 12–15 minutes

If you are short of time, you can use a ready-made pizza base.

2 tbsp extra virgin olive oil
1 garlic clove, sliced
1 tsp chopped fresh rosemary
125 g (4 oz) mushrooms, thickly sliced
75 g (3 oz) cooked chicken, shredded
100 g (3½ oz) mozzarella, finely chopped

Basic pizza dough:
250 g (8 oz) plain flour, plus extra for dusting
1½ tsp fast-acting yeast
125 ml (4 fl oz) warm water
1 tbsp extra virgin olive oil
salt and pepper

crisp green salad, to serve

Preheat the oven to 230°C/450°F/Gas Mark 8 and place a large baking tray on the centre shelf to heat up.

Make the pizza dough: sift the flour and ½ teaspoon salt into a bowl, stir in the yeast and make a well in the centre. Gradually work in the water and oil to form a soft dough, transfer to a lightly floured surface and knead the dough for 8–10 minutes until smooth and elastic. Shape into a ball and place in an oiled bowl, cover with cling film and leave the dough to rise in a warm place for 45 minutes or until doubled in size.

Heat the oil in a frying pan, add the garlic and rosemary and stir-fry for 30 seconds. Add the mushrooms and cook over a high heat for 3–4 minutes until lightly golden. Set aside.

Divide the dough in half and roll out each half to a 23 cm/9 in round. Press the dough into 2 shallow tins (the same size as the dough) and top each one with half the mushroom mixture, the chicken and mozzarella. Season with a little salt and pepper and bake on the heated baking tray for 12–15 minutes until bubbling and golden. Serve hot with a green salad.

CHICKEN AND FRESH HERB BAGUETTES

Serves: 2
Preparation time: 5 minutes
Cooking time: 5 minutes

2 tbsp extra virgin olive oil
2 skinless chicken breast fillets, thinly sliced
2 garlic cloves, crushed
grated zest and juice of 2 limes
salt and pepper
1 medium or 2 small French sticks
a handful of fresh basil, mint and coriander leaves

sweet chilli sauce, to serve

Heat the oil in a non-stick frying pan and stir-fry the chicken for 2–3 minutes until lightly golden. Add the garlic and lime zest and fry for a further 1 minute. Remove from the heat and add the lime juice, salt and pepper.

Cut the French stick almost in half and fill with the herbs. Carefully tip in the hot chicken and all the pan juices. Serve hot, drizzled with a little sweet chilli sauce.

CHICKEN, BACON AND RICE BAKE

Serves 2
Preparation time: 15 minutes
Cooking time: 1 hour, plus 5 minutes resting

Don't forget to remove the cocktail sticks, before serving the chicken.

> 2 skinless chicken thighs (about 175 g/6 oz each)
> 2 rashers streaky bacon, rind removed
> 1 tbsp olive oil
> 1 small onion, finely chopped
> 1 garlic clove, crushed
> 125 g (4 oz) long-grain rice
> $1/2$ tsp ground turmeric
> zest and juice $1/2$ lemon
> 250 ml (8 fl oz) chicken stock
> 1 tbsp chopped fresh coriander
> salt and pepper

Preheat the oven to 180°C/350°F/Gas Mark 4. Lay the bacon flat, place a chicken thigh at one end and roll up to enclose the meat, secure in place with cocktail sticks.

Heat the oil in a frying pan and fry the chicken for 5 minutes until browned all over, remove with a slotted spoon and set aside. Add the onion and garlic to the pan and fry gently for 5 minutes, add the rice and stir-fry for 1 minute. Stir in the turmeric, lemon zest, stock and some salt and pepper.

Transfer the rice mixture to a small baking dish, arrange the chicken thighs over the top, pressing down gently. Cover with a double layer of foil and bake for 45-50 minutes until the rice and chicken are cooked.

Remove from the oven and stir in the lemon juice and coriander, cover and rest for 5 minutes before serving. Remove the cocktail sticks.

WARM CHICKEN AND CHICKPEA PILAFF

Serves: 2
Preparation time: 10 minutes
Cooking time: 15 minutes

This North African dish can be served as a main course with rice or as part of a spread.

2 tbsp extra virgin olive oil, plus extra for drizzling
1 small onion, chopped
1 garlic clove, chopped
1 tsp freshly grated root ginger
1 tsp ground coriander
$1/2$ tsp ground cumin
a pinch of dried red chilli flakes
1 x 400 g (13 oz) can chickpeas, drained
2 tomatoes, roughly chopped
250 g (8 oz) cooked chicken, shredded
juice of $1^{1}/2$ lemons
salt and pepper
1 tbsp chopped fresh coriander

Heat the oil in a frying pan and gently fry the onion, garlic, ginger and spices for 10 minutes until the onion is softened. Add the chickpeas, tomatoes, chicken, lemon juice and salt and pepper, cover and cook for 5 minutes.

Remove from the heat, stir in the coriander, adjust seasonings and serve drizzled with a little extra olive oil.

GREEN CHICKEN CURRY

Serves: 2
Preparation time: 10 minutes
Cooking time: 15 minutes

Each double Kaffir lime leaf should be counted as 2 separate leaves, so for this recipe take 3 leaves and separate into 6.

1 tbsp sunflower oil
1 tbsp green curry paste
6 Kaffir lime leaves, torn
1 tbsp Thai fish sauce
2 tsp soft brown sugar
400 ml (14 fl oz) coconut milk
350 g (12 oz) skinless chicken thigh, sliced
125 g (4 oz) can bamboo shoots, drained
125 g (4 oz) baby corn, halved lengthways
a large handful of Thai basil leaves or coriander leaves
1 tbsp lime juice

boiled jasmine rice, to serve

Heat the oil in a wok or large frying pan, add the curry paste and lime leaves and stir-fry for 1–2 minutes until fragrant. Add the fish sauce, sugar and coconut milk, bring to the boil and simmer gently for 5 minutes.

Add the chicken and cook for 5 minutes. Add the bamboo shoots and corn and cook for a further 3 minutes. Stir through the basil or coriander leaves and lime juice and serve with plain boiled jasmine rice.

CHICKEN NOODLE SOUP

Serves: 4
Preparation time: 10 minutes
Cooking time: 18 minutes

Thai basil has a more aniseed flavour than ordinary basil (which can be used instead) and is available from specialist greengrocers and Asian food stores.

600 ml (1 pint) fresh chicken stock
300 ml ($^1/_2$ pint) water
1 stalk lemongrass, chopped
6 Kaffir lime leaves, torn
2 small skinless chicken breast fillets, trimmed (about
   150 g/5 oz each)
juice of 1 lime
100 g (3$^1/_2$ oz) dried egg thread noodles
1 red bird's eye chilli, seeded and sliced
a few fresh Thai basil, mint and coriander leaves

Put the stock, water, lemongrass and lime leaves in a saucepan, bring to a very gentle simmer, add the chicken breasts and poach for 10 minutes, without allowing the water to boil (or it will become cloudy).

Remove the chicken with a slotted spoon, cool slightly and cut into thick slices. Bring the stock to the boil, simmer gently for 5 minutes and stir in the lime juice.

Cook the noodles according to the packet instructions. Place the noodles in warmed bowls, add the sliced chicken, chilli and herbs and strain over the stock. Serve hot.

HOISIN CHICKEN WINGS

Serves: 2
Preparation time: 10 minutes
Cooking time: 45–50 minutes

> 3 tbsp hoisin sauce
> 2 tbsp dark soy sauce
> 1 tbsp lime juice
> 1 tbsp clear honey
> 1 garlic clove, crushed
> 1/4 tsp Chinese five-spice powder
> 6 large chicken wings

Preheat the oven to 200°C/400°F/Gas Mark 6 and line a roasting tin with foil. Mix the hoisin sauce, soy sauce, lime juice, honey, garlic and Chinese five-spice in a bowl, stirring well until combined. Place the chicken wings in the prepared tin, add the sauce and stir well to coat the wings evenly.

Roast the chicken for 45–50 minutes, stirring every 15 minutes or so until it is golden and sticky. Cool before serving.

COCONUT CHICKEN

Serves: 2
Preparation time: 15 minutes
Cooking time: 5 minutes

150 ml ($\frac{1}{4}$ pint) coconut cream
3 tbsp smooth peanut butter
1$\frac{1}{2}$ tbsp light soy sauce
1 tbsp lime juice
1 tbsp soft brown sugar
2 tbsp vegetable oil
350 g (12 oz) skinless chicken breast fillet, sliced
2 large red chillies, seeded and sliced
125 g (4 oz) mangetout, trimmed
a handful of fresh coriander leaves

boiled rice, to serve

Place the coconut cream, peanut butter, soy sauce, lime juice and sugar in a saucepan and heat gently, stirring until the peanut butter is melted and the sauce smooth. Bring to the boil and immediately remove from the heat.

Heat the oil in a wok or frying pan, add the chicken and stir-fry for 2 minutes until lightly golden. Add the chillies and mangetout and fry for a further 1 minute. Add the sauce, toss well and heat through for 30 seconds.

Garnish the chicken with coriander leaves and serve with boiled rice.

CHICKEN AND ASPARAGUS WITH CAPER BUTTER

Serves 2
Preparation time: 10 minutes, plus chilling
Cooking time: 10 minutes

The best way to test if the chicken is cooked through is to insert a metal skewer into the centre. Leave it for 30 seconds, remove and test the skewer with a fingertip – if it is hot then the chicken is cooked, if cold, allow the chicken to cook a little longer.

1 tbsp extra virgin olive oil
2 skinless chicken breast fillets
250 g (8 oz) asparagus spears

Caper butter:
50 g (2 oz) unsalted butter, softened
2 tbsp capers in brine, drained and washed
$^{1}/_{2}$ tbsp chopped parsley
grated zest of $^{1}/_{2}$ unwaxed lemon
salt and pepper

Make the caper butter: place all the ingredients in a food processor and process until smooth and evenly blended. Transfer to a small piece of foil, roll into a log and chill for 30 minutes. Remove from the fridge and cut into slices.

Heat the oil in a frying pan and fry the chicken breasts for 6–7 minutes each side or until golden and cooked through. Remove the chicken from the pan and wrap loosely in foil. Rest for 5 minutes.

Steam or boil the asparagus for 3–4 minutes until tender. Arrange the asparagus on plates, top with the chicken and a couple of slices of the caper butter.

PAN-FRIED CHICKEN WITH CHERRY TOMATO SAUCE

Serves: 2
Preparation time: 5 minutes
Cooking time: 20 minutes

2 skinless chicken breast fillets
salt and pepper
15 g (1/2 oz) butter
1 tbsp extra virgin olive oil
1 garlic clove, sliced
250 g (8 oz) cherry tomatoes, halved
1 tbsp balsamic vinegar
a few fresh basil leaves

spinach salad, to serve

Season the chicken with salt and pepper. Heat the butter and oil in a frying pan and as soon as the foam dies down add the chicken. Cook for 6–7 minutes each side until golden and cooked through. Remove the chicken from the pan, wrap loosely in foil and rest for 5 minutes.

Add the garlic to the pan and fry for 1 minute. Add the tomatoes and vinegar, cover and cook gently for 5 minutes until softened. Stir in any chicken juices collected in the foil, garnish with the basil leaves and serve with a spinach salad.

CHILLI CHICKEN PASTA WITH ROCKET

Serves: 2
Preparation time: 5 minutes
Cooking time: 12–15 minutes

250 g (8 oz) dried penne or fusilli
4 tbsp extra virgin olive oil
250 g (8 oz) skinless chicken breast fillet, sliced
2 garlic cloves, crushed
a pinch of dried red chilli flakes
grated zest and juice of $^1/_2$ unwaxed lemon
100 g (3$^1/_2$ oz) large rocket leaves
a handful of fresh basil leaves
salt and pepper

shaved Parmesan, to serve

Cook the pasta according to the packet instructions until al dente (just cooked). Drain well, reserving 2 tablespoons of the cooking water, and return to the pan.

Heat the oil in a large frying pan and fry the chicken for 5 minutes. Add the garlic, chilli and lemon zest and fry for a further 3–4 minutes until the chicken is cooked through.

Add the pasta to the pan with the reserved water, lemon juice, rocket, basil and salt and pepper. Stir over a medium heat for 1–2 minutes until the rocket is just wilted. Serve garnished with plenty of shaved Parmesan.

CHICKEN AND LEEK PIES

Serves: 2
Preparation time: 20 minutes, plus cooling
Cooking time: 30 minutes

You will have some puff pastry left over; simply wrap in cling film and freeze for later use in another dish.

25 g (1 oz) butter
1 leek, trimmed and sliced
1½ tbsp plain flour
75 ml (3 fl oz) chicken stock
75 ml (3 fl oz) single cream
225 g (7½ oz) cooked chicken, diced
1 tbsp chopped fresh tarragon
salt and pepper
1 x 400 g (13 oz) block puff pastry
1 egg, lightly beaten

plain flour, for dusting

Melt the butter in a saucepan and fry the leek for 5 minutes. Add the flour, stir well and then gradually stir in the chicken stock and cream and cook gently for 1 minute until thickened. Stir in the chicken, tarragon and some salt and pepper and remove from the heat. Divide the chicken mixture between 2 x 250 ml (8 fl oz) pie dishes and leave to cool for 30 minutes.

Preheat the oven to 200°C/400°F/Gas Mark 6. Cut the pastry in half, freeze one half and then cut the remaining pastry in half again. Roll each piece out on a lightly floured surface to a round 2.5 cm (1 in) larger than the pie tins.

Brush the rim of each pie dish with a little beaten egg, top with the pastry, pressing down around the edges to seal in the filling. Using a sharp knife, cut around the dish to trim the excess pastry.

Brush the surface of the pastry lightly with beaten egg and pierce a small hole in the centre of each pie. Place on a baking tray and bake for 20–25 minutes until the pastry is puffed up and golden.

POUSSIN WITH PESTO BUTTER

Serves: 2
Preparation time: 10 minutes
Cooking time: 30 minutes

Poussin makes a good alternative to chicken especially when serving two as there will be no leftovers to worry about. There will be some pesto butter left over, so wrap in foil and freeze for up to 1 month. Thaw for 1 hour and use as required.

$^{1}/_{2}$ lemon, halved
2 x 500 g (1 lb) poussin
65 g (2$^{1}/_{2}$ oz) unsalted butter, softened
$^{1}/_{2}$ bunch of fresh basil
1 small garlic clove, crushed
1 tbsp pine nuts
2 tbsp freshly grated Parmesan
salt and pepper

Preheat the oven to 200°C/400°F/Gas Mark 6. Stuff a lemon quarter into the cavity of each poussin. Starting at the neck end of each bird carefully push your fingers between the skin and flesh up towards the tip of the breast and drumsticks to form a pocket.

Place the butter, basil, garlic, pine nuts, Parmesan and salt and pepper in a food processor and process until smooth. Reserving half the butter for another time, push the rest into the prepared pocket, smoothing flat.

Place the poussin in a small roasting tin and cook for 30 minutes. Remove from the oven and rest for 5 minutes before serving.

CHICKEN BURGER WITH SATAY SAUCE

Serves: 2
Preparation time: 20 minutes, plus marinating
Cooking time: 6–8 minutes

2 small skinless chicken breast fillets,
    trimmed (125 g/4 oz each)
2 tsp peanut oil
1 garlic clove, crushed
1 tsp ground turmeric
1 tbsp sweet chilli sauce
salt

Satay sauce:
2 tbsp smooth peanut butter
1 tbsp coconut cream
1 tbsp sweet chilli sauce
1 tbsp lime juice
1 tsp light soy sauce
1 tsp soft brown sugar
salt

To serve:
2 burger buns
sliced cucumber
sliced tomato
fresh coriander leaves

Lay the chicken breast flat on a board and, using a sharp knife, slice almost completely in half horizontally through the thickest side, and open out flat.

Combine the remaining ingredients and a little salt in a bowl and rub all over the chicken. Leave to marinate for 30 minutes.

Make the satay sauce: combine all the ingredients in a small saucepan and heat gently until smooth. Set aside to cool.

Preheat the grill to high and cook the chicken for 3–4 minutes each side until lightly charred and cooked through.

Toast the burger buns and fill each with the cooked chicken, cucumber, tomato, coriander and the satay sauce.

ASIAN-STYLE BRAISED CHICKEN AND MUSHROOMS

Serves: 2
Preparation time: 15 minutes
Cooking time: 10 minutes

2 tbsp extra virgin olive oil
350 g (12 oz) skinless chicken breast fillet, sliced
a pinch of salt
250 g (8 oz) mixed mushrooms, such as button,
    shiitake and oyster
2 garlic cloves, crushed
25 g (1 oz) butter, diced
50 ml (2 fl oz) dry white wine
4 spring onions, thickly sliced
1 tbsp light soy sauce
1 tbsp chopped fresh coriander

cooked Chinese egg thread noodles, to serve

Heat the oil in a wok or large frying pan until hot. Carefully add the chicken and salt and stir-fry for 2–3 minutes until browned. Remove with a slotted spoon and set aside.

Add the mushrooms and garlic to the pan, stir once and then dot over the butter. Cover and cook over a medium heat for 5 minutes. Remove the lid, add the wine, spring onions and soy sauce, stir once and cook for a further 2–3 minutes. Return the chicken to the pan, add the coriander and cook for a final 1 minute. Serve with freshly cooked noodles.

MOZZARELLA-STUFFED CHICKEN WITH SPICY TOMATO SAUCE

Serves: 2
Preparation time: 20 minutes
Cooking time: 30 minutes

4 skinless chicken breast fillets
50 g (2 oz) mozzarella, sliced
4 basil leaves
4 slices Parma ham
25 g (1 oz) butter

Spicy tomato sauce:
1 x 400 g (13 oz) can chopped tomatoes
1 tbsp extra virgin olive oil
1 large garlic clove, crushed
$1/2$ tsp dried red chilli flakes
1 tsp caster sugar
1 tbsp chopped fresh basil
salt and pepper

Make the tomato sauce: put all the ingredients into a saucepan and bring to the boil. Simmer gently for about 20 minutes or until the sauce is thickened. Keep warm.

Lay the chicken breast fillets on a chopping board and, using a sharp knife, cut a deep pocket into the thickest side, running the knife almost through the breast but leaving it whole. Place 2 slices of the mozzarella and 2 basil leaves into each pocket and then wrap each breast in 2 slices of Parma ham, securing it with a cocktail stick.

Heat the butter in a saucepan and as soon as it stops foaming add the chicken breasts. Fry over a medium heat for 6–7 minutes each side until the chicken is cooked through and the cheese is oozing out. Serve with the tomato sauce.

PORK, BEEF AND LAMB

With a variety of kinds and cuts of meat included in your week's shop and your basic store cupboard you can make any one of the dishes shown below. The fresh ingredients that you will need are highlighted in the fridge. Some recipes need extra ingredients or vegetables to serve which are on the shopping list. Always read through the recipe you choose to make sure that you have all the ingredients to hand.

GREEN BEANS
FRENCH BEANS
SUGAR SNAP PEAS
ONION
SHALLOTS
GARLIC
POTATOES
MIXED FRESH HERBS
FRESH ROOT GINGER
CHIVES
BABY SPINACH
MIXED ASIAN LEAVES
PINE NUTS
PISTACHIO NUTS
ROASTED CASHEWS
BLACK OLIVES
SESAME SEEDS
SWEET CHILLI SAUCE
OYSTER SAUCE
CHILLI BEAN SAUCE
MEDIUM CURRY PASTE
TOMATO KETCHUP
TOMATO CHUTNEY
MANGO CHUTNEY
WORCESTERSHIRE SAUCE
DIJON MUSTARD
WHOLEGRAIN MUSTARD
SESAME OIL
PEANUT OIL
SHERRY VINEGAR
CHINESE RICE WINE OR DRY SHERRY
MARSALA
RED WINE
CLEAR HONEY
INSTANT POLENTA
CHINESE EGG THREAD NOODLES
MIDDLE EASTERN FLAT BREADS
PUY LENTILS
RAISINS
FROZEN PUFF PASTRY
FROZEN SHORT CRUST PASTRY
FROZEN PEAS
CHORIZO SAUSAGE
HUMMUS
BAMBOO SKEWERS
CANNED BUTTER BEANS

GAMMON STEAKS WITH PINEAPPLE SALSA

Serves: 2
Preparation time: 10 minutes
Cooking time: 6–8 minutes

1 tbsp Dijon mustard
1 tbsp clear honey
2 x 250 g (8 oz) gammon steaks

Pineapple salsa:
$1/4$ pineapple (about 150g/5oz) finely diced
1 small garlic clove, crushed
1 large red chilli, deseeded and diced
juice of $1/2$ lime
1 tbsp chopped fresh coriander
3 tbsp extra virgin olive oil
salt and pepper

Make the salsa: combine the pineapple, garlic, chilli, lime juice, coriander and olive oil in a bowl and season to taste. Set aside to infuse.

Preheat the grill to high. Combine the mustard and honey, brush over the steaks and grill for 3–4 minutes each side until cooked through. Rest for 5 minutes and serve the steaks with the pineapple salsa.

MUSTARD AND ROSEMARY PORK WITH APPLES

Serves: 2
Preparation time: 5 minutes, plus marinating
Cooking time: 12–15 minutes

1 tbsp mixed Dijon and wholegrain mustard
1 tbsp orange juice
1 tbsp extra virgin olive oil
1 tbsp chopped fresh rosemary
salt and pepper
25 g (1 oz) butter
2 x 250 g (8 oz) pork loin chops
1 large apple, cored and cut into thick wedges
50 ml (2 fl oz) apple juice

Combine the mustard, orange juice, oil, rosemary and salt and pepper in a bowl. Rub all over the pork and marinate for 30 minutes.

Heat the butter in a frying pan and, as soon as it stops foaming, add the chops and fry over a medium heat for 4–5 minutes each side until golden and cooked through. Remove from the pan and wrap loosely in foil. Rest for 5 minutes.

Add the apples to the pan and fry gently for 2 minutes until golden on both sides. Add the apple juice to the pan and simmer for 1–2 minutes until the sauce is thickened slightly. Stir in any pork juices from the foil and serve the chops with the apples and sauce.

43

STIR-FRIED PORK WITH PAK CHOI AND NOODLES

Serves: 2
Preparation time: 10 minutes
Cooking time: 3–4 minutes

Pak choi is a Chinese green vegetable used in stir-fries and soups. It is widely available from supermarkets and greengrocers.

250 g (8 oz) pak choi
50 ml (2 fl oz) Chinese rice wine (or dry sherry)
2 tbsp oyster sauce
2 tbsp light soy sauce
2 tbsp sweet chilli sauce
2 tbsp water
2 tsp sesame oil
250 g (8 oz) dried Chinese egg thread noodles
3 tbsp vegetable oil
2 garlic cloves, sliced
250 g (8 oz) pork tenderloin, sliced thinly
4 spring onions, trimmed and thickly sliced
2 cm ($\frac{1}{2}$ in) piece of root ginger, peeled and shredded

Wash the pak choi, cut into thick slices and dry thoroughly on kitchen paper. Mix together the rice wine, oyster sauce, soy sauce, chilli sauce, water and sesame oil. Set aside.

Cook the noodles according to the packet instructions, drain well and keep warm.

Heat half the vegetable oil in a wok or large frying pan and fry the pak choi and garlic for 1 minute, then transfer to a plate. Add the remaining oil to the pan and stir-fry the pork for 2 minutes until browned. Add the spring onions and ginger and stir-fry for 30 seconds. Add the oyster sauce mixture and stir-fry for a further 1 minute. Finally return the pak choi to the pan and stir-fry for 30 seconds.

Place the noodles in bowls and serve topped with the pork mixture.

PORK WITH SHERRY VINEGAR, RAISINS AND PINE NUTS

Serves: 2
Preparation time: 5 minutes
Cooking time: 7–8 minutes

Sherry vinegar has a wonderfully pungent flavour and is available from some larger supermarkets and delis. Balsamic makes a good substitute.

2 x 250 g (8 oz) pork loin chops
salt and pepper
1 tbsp extra virgin olive oil
15 g ($\frac{1}{2}$ oz) butter
100 ml (3$\frac{1}{2}$ fl oz) sweet sherry
2 tbsp sherry vinegar
50 g (2 oz) raisins
1 tbsp chopped fresh parsley
2 tbsp pine nuts

baby spinach leaves, to serve

46

Season the pork chops with salt and pepper. Heat the oil and butter in a heavy-based frying pan and, as soon as the butter stops foaming, fry the chops for 4–5 minutes each side. Remove from the pan, wrap loosely in foil and rest for 5 minutes.

Lower the heat, add the sherry to the pan and cook for 2–3 minutes until reduced by about half, then add the vinegar, raisins, parsley and pine nuts and cook for 1 minute. Serve the chops with the sauce and baby spinach leaves.

CHORIZO RAGU WITH WET POLENTA

Serves: 2
Preparation time: 20 minutes
Cooking time: 30 minutes

Chorizo is a spicy sausage used in Spanish cooking. To mince it, chop roughly and place in a food processor and pulse until finely minced.

1 tbsp olive oil
1 small onion, finely chopped
1 garlic clove, crushed
250 g (8 oz) chorizo sausage, minced
2 rashers smoked back bacon, diced
1 x 400 g (13 oz) can chopped tomatoes
1 tsp dried oregano
salt and pepper

Polenta:
750 ml (1^1/$_2$ pints) water
100 g (3^1/$_2$ oz) instant polenta
25 g (1 oz) butter
25 g (1 oz) freshly grated Parmesan cheese
salt and pepper

freshly grated Parmesan, to serve

Heat the oil in a saucepan and fry the onion and garlic for 5 minutes. Add the chorizo and bacon and fry for a further 5 minutes. Add the tomatoes and oregano, bring to the boil and simmer gently, uncovered, for 20 minutes until thickened. Season to taste and keep warm.

Pour the water in to a pan and bring to a rolling ball with 1 teaspoon of salt. Gradually whisk in the polenta in a steady stream and cook, stirring, over a low heat for 5 minutes until the polenta has thickened and is beginning to leave the sides of the pan. Remove from the heat and beat in the butter, cheese and seasonings to taste.

Spoon the polenta into shallow bowls, spoon over the sausage ragu and serve topped with grated Parmesan.

PORK WITH MARSALA
AND BUTTERY SPINACH

Serves: 2
Preparation time: 10 minutes
Cooking time: 15 minutes

Marsala is a fortified wine from Sicily. It has a rich almost herb-like aroma. It is available from all good wine stores.

> 250 g (8 oz) spinach leaves, washed
> 2 x 200 g (7 oz) pork loin chops
> 1 tsp chopped fresh thyme
> salt and pepper
> 1 tbsp extra virgin olive oil
> 40 g (1$\frac{1}{2}$ oz) butter
> 1 tbsp Marsala
> 50 ml (2 fl oz) fresh orange juice
> pinch of grated nutmeg

Place the wet spinach leaves into a saucepan and heat gently, stirring for 1–2 minutes until just wilted. Drain well and set aside.

Rub the pork all over with thyme, salt and pepper. Heat the oil and 15g/$\frac{1}{2}$ oz of the butter in a large frying pan and, as soon as the butter stops foaming, fry the pork for 4–5 minutes each side until browned and cooked through. Wrap loosely in foil and rest for 5 minutes.

Add the Marsala to the pan, stir once and then add the orange juice, simmer for 5 minutes until the sauce is reduced and thickened.

Melt the remaining butter in a saucepan and gently fry the spinach for 2–3 minutes until heated through. Season with nutmeg, salt and pepper. Serve with the pork chops and Marsala sauce and spinach.

TOAD-IN-THE-HOLE

Serves: 2
Preparation time: 5 minutes
Cooking time: 35 minutes

A loaf tin is the ideal container for 2 servings of toad-in-the-hole.

> 60 g (2$^{1}/_{2}$ oz) plain flour
> pinch of salt
> 150 ml ($^{1}/_{4}$ pint) milk
> 1 large egg, beaten
> 1 tsp chopped fresh thyme
> 4 tbsp sunflower oil
> 4 good quality sausages (whatever flavour you like)
>
> tomato ketchup, to serve

Preheat the oven to 230°C/450°F/Gas Mark 8. Sift the flour and a pinch of salt into a bowl and gradually whisk in the milk and egg to form a smooth batter. Add the thyme and transfer to a jug.

Pour the oil into a 1 kg/2 lb loaf tin and place in the oven for 5 minutes until really hot. Carefully add the sausages, using a pair of tongs as the oil may spit, and bake for 10 minutes until the sausages are starting to brown.

Remove the tin from the oven and, again being very careful, pour in the batter. Immediately return the tin to the oven and bake for 20 minutes until the batter is risen and set. Serve with tomato ketchup.

PEPPER STEAK WITH SHOESTRING CHIPS

Serves: 2
Preparation time: 15 minutes
Cooking time: 2–3 minutes

Make sure you cut the potatoes as thinly as possible, both into slices and again into sticks to give them that shoestring appearance and lovely crisp texture.

350 g (12 oz) main crop potatoes, such as Desiree or
    King Edwards
2 x 250 g (8 oz) beef rib eye steaks
sea salt
2 tsp coarsely ground black peppercorns
15 g ($^{1}/_{2}$ oz) butter
1 tbsp extra virgin olive oil
50 ml (2 fl oz) red wine
100 ml ($3^{1}/_{2}$ fl oz) beef stock

sunflower oil, for deep frying

Peel the potatoes and cut lengthways into wafer-thin slices. Then cut the slices into thin strips. Place in a sieve and wash under cold water to remove excess starch. Dry the potato strips thoroughly on kitchen paper. Set aside.

Rub the steaks with the sea salt and ground peppercorns. Heat the butter and oil in a frying pan and, as soon as the butter stops foaming, fry the steaks for 3–4 minutes each side for rare, 4–5 minutes each side for medium or 6 minutes each side for well done. Wrap the steaks in foil and rest for 5 minutes. Add the wine to the frying pan, stir well and simmer for 1 minute. Add the stock and simmer for 2–3 minutes until the sauce is reduced and thickened. Keep warm.

Heat 5 cm/2 in sunflower oil in a deep saucepan until a small cube of bread crisps in 30 seconds. Deep-fry the potatoes in batches over a medium heat for 2–3 minutes until crisp and golden. Remove with a slotted spoon and drain on kitchen paper. Serve the steaks with the pan juices and the shoestring chips.

STEAK WITH MUSTARD CRÈME FRAÎCHE

Serves: 2
Preparation time: 5 minutes
Cooking time: 10 minutes

2 x 250 g (8 oz) beef rib-eye steaks
15 g ($^1/_2$ oz) butter
1 tbsp extra virgin olive oil
50 g (2 oz) crème fraîche
1 tbsp wholegrain mustard
1 tbsp chopped fresh chives
salt and pepper

Season the steaks with salt and pepper. Heat the butter and oil together in a frying pan until the butter stops foaming. Add the steaks and cook for 3–4 minutes on each side for rare, 4–5 minutes each side for medium and 6 minutes each side for well done. Remove the steaks from the pan and wrap loosely in foil.

Return the pan to the heat, add the crème fraîche and mustard and, using a spatula, scrape any bits of meat from the base of the pan. Simmer the sauce gently for 2–3 minutes until thickened. Add the chives, season to taste and spoon over the steaks.

THAI BEEF SALAD

Serves: 2
Preparation time: 15 minutes, plus cooling
Cooking time: 5 minutes

Szechuan pepper is a Chinese spice with a particularly fragrant flavour. It is available from the spice section of supermarkets.

1 large beef fillet steak (about 350g/12 oz)
1 tsp sesame oil
salt
$1/2$ tsp crushed Szechuan peppercorns
1 tbsp Thai fish sauce
1 tbsp lime juice
1 tbsp soft brown sugar
1 bag mixed Asian salad leaves
1 small cucumber, thinly sliced
2 spring onions, thinly sliced
1 large red chilli, deseeded and sliced
25 g (1 oz) mixed herbs, such as Thai basil, mint and
   coriander leaves
1 tbsp roasted cashews, finely chopped

Brush the steak with the oil and rub all over with the Szechuan pepper and some salt. Heat a ridged grill pan until hot, add the beef and cook for 1 minute each side. Remove from the pan and leave to cool. Cut into thin slices.

Heat the fish sauce, lime juice and sugar in a small saucepan until the sugar dissolves. Set aside to cool.

Combine the beef, salad leaves, cucumber, onions, chilli and herbs in a large bowl, add the dressing and toss well until evenly coated. Divide between serving plates and top with the cashew nuts.

CHILLI BEEF WITH PAK CHOI AND SESAME

Serves: 2
Preparation time: 10 minutes, plus marinating
Cooking time: 5 minutes

Chilli bean sauce is a thick reddish paste available from Asian food stores and some larger supermarkets. Substitute hoisin sauce if unavailable.

2 tbsp light soy sauce
1 tbsp chilli bean sauce
2 tsp clear honey
1 tsp sesame oil
350 g (12 oz) beef fillet steak, thinly sliced
2 tbsp peanut oil
250 g (8 oz) baby pak choi, roughly sliced
1 small red pepper, deseeded and sliced
2 garlic cloves, sliced
1 tbsp sesame seeds, toasted

plain boiled rice, to serve

Combine the soy sauce, chilli bean sauce, honey, sesame oil and beef slices in a bowl and leave to marinate for 30 minutes. Carefully remove the meat from the marinade using a slotted spoon, shaking off excess liquid. Reserve the marinade.

Heat half the oil in a wok or deep frying pan, add the beef and stir-fry for 1–2 minutes until golden. Transfer the beef and pan juices to a plate, wipe the pan clean and return to the heat.

Add the remaining oil to the pan and stir-fry the pak choi, red pepper and garlic for 2 minutes. Return the beef and juices to the pan with the reserved marinade and heat through. Scatter over the sesame seeds and serve at once with boiled rice.

OREGANO BEEF WITH TOMATO AND FETA SALSA

Serves: 2
Preparation time: 15 minutes
Cooking time: 8 minutes

2 x 250 g (8 oz) beef fillet or sirloin steaks
$1/2$ tbsp olive oil
$1 1/2$ tbsp dried oregano
salt and pepper

Tomato and feta salsa:
2 tomatoes, deseeded and diced
1 garlic clove, crushed
1 shallot, finely chopped
50 g (2 oz) feta, diced
40 g ($1 1/2$ oz) pitted black olives
4 tbsp extra virgin olive oil
1 tbsp red wine vinegar
2 tsp fresh oregano leaves

green salad, to serve

Rub the steaks with the oil, oregano and salt and pepper and set aside.
Combine all the ingredients for the salsa in a bowl and season to taste.
Heat a ridged grill pan until hot, add the beef and fry for 3–4 minutes each side for rare, 4–5 minutes each side for medium and 6 minutes each side for well done. Rest for 5 minutes and serve topped with the salsa and a green salad.

INDIVIDUAL COTTAGE PIE

Serves: 2
Preparation time: 25 minutes
Cooking time: 1¼ hours

2 tbsp olive oil
350 g (12 oz) lean minced beef
1 small onion, finely chopped
1 small carrot, finely chopped
1 small celery stick, finely chopped
salt and pepper
300 ml (½ pint) beef stock
4 tbsp tomato purée
1 tbsp Worcestershire sauce
500 g (1 lb) main crop potatoes, such as Desiree or King
    Edwards
50 g (2 oz) butter
50 g (2 oz) grated Cheddar cheese

steamed green beans, to serve

Preheat the oven to 180°C/350°F/Gas Mark 4. Heat half the oil in a saucepan and stir-fry the mince over a high heat for 2–3 minutes until browned. Remove from the pan and set aside.

Add the remaining oil to the pan and gently fry the onion, carrot, celery and salt and pepper for 10 minutes until the vegetables are softened. Return the beef to the pan and stir in the stock, tomato purée and Worcestershire sauce. Bring to the boil, cover and simmer gently for 30 minutes. Divide the mixture between two 600 ml (1 pint) pie dishes.

Boil the potatoes for 15 minutes until tender. Drain well and return to the pan, add the butter and half the cheese and mash until smooth. Season to taste.

Spread the mash over the mince, fluff up the top with a fork and scatter over the remaining cheese. Bake for 30 minutes until the top is crisp and golden and the juices are bubbling up around the sides. Serve with steamed green beans.

LAMB STEAKS WITH BUTTER BEANS AND GREMOLATA

Serves: 2
Preparation time: 10 minutes
Cooking time: 15 minutes

2 rashers smoked streaky bacon, roughly chopped
1^1/$_2$ tbsp extra virgin olive oil, plus extra to drizzle
1 onion, chopped
^{1}/$_2$ tbsp chopped fresh sage
2 ripe tomatoes, deseeded and chopped
1 x 400 g (13 oz) can butter beans, drained
2 x 250 g (8 oz) lamb leg steaks
salt and pepper

Gremolata:
1 tbsp chopped fresh parsley
1 garlic clove, crushed
grated zest of ^{1}/$_2$ unwaxed lemon
salt and pepper

Make the gremolata by mixing together the parsley, garlic, lemon zest and salt and pepper and set aside until required.

Heat a heavy-based frying pan until hot, add the bacon and fry for 3–4 minutes until golden and the fat has started to melt. Add 1 tablespoon of the oil and fry the onions and sage for 5 minutes until softened. Add the tomatoes and beans, stir well, cover and cook gently for 5 minutes.

Rub the steaks with the remaining oil and season with salt and pepper. Heat a ridged grill pan until hot and fry the lamb for 3–4 minutes each side for rare, 4–5 minutes each side for medium or 6 minutes each side for well done.

Rest the lamb for 5 minutes and serve with the bean mixture, the gremolata and a drizzle of oil.

CURRIED MEAT PIES

Makes: 4 individual pies
Preparation time: 25 minutes, plus cooling
Cooking time: 45 minutes

This recipe makes four pies, so leave to cool and then wrap the two extra pies in foil. Freeze for later use. Puff pastry is available fresh from the chilled cabinet of most larger supermarkets.

1 tbsp olive oil
1 onion, finely chopped
350 g (12 oz) lamb mince
1 tbsp plain flour
1 x 400 g (13 oz) can chopped tomatoes
1 tbsp medium curry paste
175 g (6 oz) frozen peas
125 ml ($^1/_4$ pint) beef stock
salt and pepper
1 x 375 g (12 oz) block shortcrust pastry
1 x 375 g (12 oz) block puff pastry, thawed
1 egg, lightly beaten

spray oil, for greasing
flour, for dusting

Heat the oil in a frying pan and fry the onion for 5 minutes. Add the mince and fry for a further 5 minutes until browned. Stir in the flour, cook for 30 seconds, then stir in the tomatoes, curry paste, peas and stock. Bring to the boil and simmer for 10 minutes until thickened. Season to taste. Remove from the heat and leave the mixture to cool completely.

Preheat the oven to 220°C/425°F/Gas Mark 7 and place a baking tray in the oven to heat up. Spray four 15 cm (6 in) pie tins with oil. Cut the shortcrust pastry into quarters and roll each out on a lightly floured surface to a round 5 cm/2 in larger than the pie dishes. Press the pastry into the dishes. Divide the puff pastry into quarters and roll each piece out thinly.

Fill the pies with the cooled mince. Brush around the rim of the pastry with beaten egg and top with the puff pastry, pressing the edges together to seal. Trim off the excess pastry with a sharp knife and cut a small slit in the centre of each pie. Brush the tops with beaten egg and bake for 25 minutes until golden. Serve with mango chutney.

FLAT BREAD LAMB PIZZA WITH FETA AND PINE NUTS

Serves 2
Preparation time: 15 minutes
Cooking time: 25–30 minutes

Flat breads are similar to pitta breads but tend to be larger and thinner. They are available from the bread section of supermarkets.

2 tbsp olive oil
1 onion, thinly sliced
2 garlic cloves, crushed
250 g (8 oz) minced lamb
1 tsp ground cinnamon
salt and pepper
2 x large Middle Eastern flat breads
2 tomatoes, chopped roughly
125 g (4 oz) feta, crumbled
25 g (1 oz) raisins
25 g (1 oz) pine nuts

green salad, to serve

Preheat the oven to 220°C/425°F/Gas Mark 7 and place a baking tray on the middle shelf to heat up. Heat the oil in a frying pan and fry the onion and garlic for 10 minutes until golden. Add the lamb and cinnamon and fry for a further 5 minutes until the meat is browned, breaking the lamb up into small pieces. Season to taste.

Place the flat breads on a work surface and top with the lamb mixture, tomatoes, feta, raisins and pine nuts. Bake one at a time on the heated baking tray for 10–15 minutes until the cheese is melted and tinged brown. Serve with a green salad.

CRUSTED LAMB CUTLETS
WITH MINTED BEANS

Serves: 2
Preparation time: 20 minutes
Cooking time: 4–6 minutes

To make fresh breadcrumbs, use day-old bread. Weigh the quantity of bread required (without crusts) and crumble into small pieces, then process in a food processor until finely ground.

6 large lamb cutlets
65 g (2$\frac{1}{2}$ oz) fresh breadcrumbs
25 g (1 oz) pine nuts, ground
1 garlic clove, crushed
1 tbsp chopped fresh parsley
25 g (1 oz) freshly grated Parmesan cheese
salt and pepper
175 g (6 oz) French beans, trimmed
a few fresh mint leaves, torn
a squeeze of lemon
1 tbsp extra virgin olive oil

olive oil, for shallow frying
tomato chutney, to serve

Preheat the oven to 160°C/325°F/Gas Mark 3. Lay the cutlets flat on a chopping board and, using a mallet or rolling pin, pound the meat as flat as possible until double the size. Combine the breadcrumbs, pine nuts, garlic, parsley, Parmesan and salt and pepper and place on a plate.

Dip the flattened lamb into the breadcrumb mix and press down well to form a crust. Heat a shallow layer of oil in a frying pan and gently fry the cutlets in batches for 2–3 minutes each side. Drain on kitchen towel and keep warm in the oven while frying the rest.

Cook the beans in a pan of lightly salted, boiling water for 3 minutes, drain well and immediately toss with the mint, lemon juice, olive oil and salt and pepper. Serve with the lamb and a tomato chutney.

LAMB KOFTA WRAPS

Serves: 2
Preparation time: 15 minutes
Cooking time: 6–8 minutes

Kofta are Middle Eastern sausage-shaped patties cooked on skewers and are great packed into pitta bread with salad and hummus.

250 g (8 oz) lamb mince
25 g (1 oz) dried breadcrumbs
1 tsp ground coriander
$\frac{1}{2}$ tsp ground cumin
$\frac{1}{2}$ tsp ground cinnamon
1 garlic clove, crushed
1 tbsp chopped fresh mint
1 egg, beaten
salt and pepper
oil, for spraying
2 large flat breads

6 bamboo skewers soaked for 30 minutes in cold water

To serve:
rocket
tomato slices
hummus

Mix the lamb, breadcrumbs, spices, mint, egg and salt and pepper together until evenly combined. Divide the mixture into six 7.5 cm (3 in) sausage patties and thread on to the soaked bamboo skewers.

Preheat a ridged grill pan (or a conventional grill) until hot, spray the sausages with oil and cook for 7–8 minutes, turning half way through until cooked thoroughly.

Arrange the flat bread on plates, top with rocket leaves, tomato slices and hummus, roll up and serve while still hot.

SUNDAY ROAST LAMB WITH HERB POTATOES

Serves: 2
Preparation time: 10 minutes
Cooking time: 50–60 minutes, plus resting

Boned and rolled lamb will take 25 minutes per 500 g/1lb to cook, with 15 minutes' resting – this applies to all lamb roasts whatever the weight. If the meat is on the bone, add an extra 5 minutes per 500 g/1 lb, plus 20 minutes' resting. The lamb will be medium rare.

> 250 g (8 oz) new potatoes
> 1 onion, cut into thin wedges
> 4 garlic cloves, unpeeled
> 2 tbsp extra virgin olive oil
> 1 tbsp roughly chopped fresh rosemary
> salt and pepper
> 1 kg (2 lb) piece boned leg (or shoulder)
> 1 tbsp plain flour
> 50 ml (2 fl oz) red wine
> 150 ml ($1/4$ pint) lamb or chicken stock

Preheat the oven to 220°C/425°F/Gas Mark 7. Cut the potatoes into thick wedges or quarters and toss with the onions, garlic, oil, rosemary and salt and pepper. Place in a roasting pan and roast for 10 minutes.

Rub the lamb with a little extra oil and season with salt and pepper. Heat a frying pan for 5 minutes until hot, add the lamb and cook for 5 minutes until browned all over. Add the lamb to the potatoes and cook for a further 30 minutes or until a skewer inserted into the centre of the meat comes out hot.

Remove the lamb to a plate, cover loosely with foil and rest for 15 minutes. Using a slotted spoon, transfer the potatoes to a dish and keep warm.

Place the roasting pan on a gentle heat, add the flour and stir for 30 seconds until bubbling and golden. Whisk in the wine and boil, stirring constantly, for 1 minute, then stir in the stock and simmer for 5 minutes. Season to taste. Carve the lamb and serve with the potatoes and gravy.

LAMB SALAD WITH PISTACHIO AND MINT PESTO

Serves: 2–3
Preparation time: 15 minutes
Cooking time: 25–30 minutes, plus cooling

Lamb tenderloin is a very tender cut of meat taken from a whole loin.
You may need to ask your butcher to prepare it for you. It is great seared
on the grill and is cooked in just a few minutes.

125 g (4 oz) puy lentils
salt
125 g (4 oz) sugar snaps, trimmed
2 x 250 g (8 oz) lamb tenderloin
salt and pepper
olive oil
a handful of baby spinach leaves

Pistachio and mint pesto:
25 g (1 oz) pistachio nuts
15 g (^{1}/$_2$ oz) fresh mint
1 garlic clove, crushed
2 spring onions, chopped
125 ml (4 fl oz) extra virgin olive oil
2 tbsp white wine vinegar

Place the lentils in a saucepan with plenty of cold water, add a little
salt and bring to the boil. Simmer for 20 minutes until tender. Drain well
and set aside to cool. Cook the sugar snap peas in a saucepan of lightly
salted boiling water for 3 minutes. Drain, refresh under cold water and
pat dry.

Season the lamb on all sides and rub with oil. Heat a ridged grill pan
until hot and sear the lamb for 2–3 minutes each side. Leave to rest for
5 minutes and cut into thin slices.

Make the pesto: place the nuts, mint, garlic and spring onions in a food
processor and process until coarsely ground. Add the oil and process again
until fairly smooth and bright green. Stir in the vinegar and season to taste.

Place the spinach leaves, sugar snap peas, lamb and lentils in a bowl,
add the pesto and toss well until evenly coated.

FISH AND SEAFOOD

You can add variety to your fish dishes with seafood like mussels and squid (not shown). The other fresh ingredients that you will need to make any of the fish recipes are highlighted in the fridge. Extra ingredients or vegetables to serve are shown on the list. Always read through the recipe you choose to make sure that you have all the ingredients to hand.

MUSSELS
SQUID
POTATOES
MANGETOUT
GREEN BEANS
FRESH ROOT GINGER
FRESH ROSEMARY
FRESH MARJORAM
LEMONGRASS
GREEN SALAD
KAFFIR LIME LEAVES
GROUND TURMERIC
RED CHILLI FLAKES
GARAM MASALA
CURRY POWDER
TOMATO KETCHUP
MUSTARD SEEDS
BAGUETTE
PITTA BREAD
CRUSTY BREAD
PARMA HAM
ANCHOVY FILLETS
CAPERS IN BRINE
CANNED CANNELLINI BEANS
COUSCOUS
RICE NOODLES
JASMINE RICE
SESAME SEEDS
SESAME OIL
CLEAR HONEY
BLANCHED ALMONDS
SAKE
MIRIN
WHITE WINE
LIGHT BEER
BLACK OLIVES
BAMBOO SKEWERS
TAPENADE
COCONUT MILK

KEDGEREE

Serves: 4
Preparation time: 10 minutes
Cooking time: 25 minutes

This recipe makes enough for 4 servings, but it keeps well and improves overnight. Store in an airtight container in the fridge.

500 g (1 lb) smoked haddock fillet
40 g (1$^{1}/_{2}$ oz) butter
1 small onion, finely chopped
grated zest and juice of 1 unwaxed lemon
1 tbsp curry powder
250 g (8 oz) long-grain rice
450 ml ($^{3}/_{4}$ pint) fish or chicken stock
2 dried bay leaves
salt and pepper
2 eggs
2 tbsp chopped fresh coriander

Cut the smoked haddock into 4 pieces. Melt the butter in a saucepan and gently fry the onion, lemon zest and curry powder for 10 minutes until the onion is really softened. Add the rice, stir-fry for 30 seconds and then add the stock, bay leaves and salt and pepper. Bring to the boil and add the smoked haddock pieces, pressing them down into the rice. Cover and cook over a very low heat for 15 minutes. Remove the pan from the heat but leave undisturbed for a further 5 minutes.

Boil the eggs for 8 minutes, then drain and refresh under cold water. Shell the eggs and chop roughly.

Remove the fish to a plate and carefully peel away and discard the skin and any bones. Roughly flake the fish and add to the rice with the coriander, chopped eggs and lemon juice. Stir gently until combined and serve warm.

SPICY TUNA AND BEAN SALAD

Serves: 2–4
Preparation time: 10 minutes
Cooking time: 2 minutes

Fresh tuna (and canned) is packed full of goodness as it is high in protein, B-vitamins and essential Omega-3 fatty acids. Tuna should always be served rare as over-cooking will make it tough.

> 1 tbsp extra virgin olive oil
> 1 tsp ground coriander
> $1/2$ tsp ground turmeric
> $1/2$ tsp ground cinnamon
> salt and pepper
> 2 x 200 g (7 oz) tuna steaks
> 1 x 400 g (13 oz) can cannellini beans, drained
> 150 g (5 oz) cucumber, deseeded and finely chopped
> 2 tomatoes, finely chopped
> 2 spring onions, finely chopped
> 2 tbsp chopped fresh herbs, such as coriander, mint and
>   parsley
>
> Chilli dressing:
> 4 tbsp extra virgin olive oil
> 1 garlic clove, crushed
> grated zest and juice of 1 unwaxed lemon
> 1 bird's eye red chilli, deseeded and diced
> salt and pepper
>
> toasted pitta bread, to serve

Combine the oil, spices and salt and pepper and brush all over the tuna steaks. Heat a ridged grill pan for 5 minutes until really hot and cook the tuna for 1 minute each side. Remove from the heat and leave to cool.

Combine the beans, cucumber, tomatoes, spring onion and herbs in a large bowl. Cut the tuna into large chunks and add to the salad.

Make the dressing: whisk the ingredients together and season to taste. Pour over the salad, toss well and serve with toasted pitta bread.

MONKFISH AND PARMA HAM WITH BALSAMIC GLAZE

Serves: 2
Preparation time: 15 minutes
Cooking time: 45–50 minutes

Boiling balsamic vinegar to a thick syrupy glaze enhances both the flavour and sweetness. Although the volume reduces by three-quarters, the resulting glaze is used sparingly, providing a delicious sauce for grilled fish or chicken. It will keep indefinitely, although mine rarely lasts long!

1 x 500 ml (15 fl oz) balsamic vinegar
2 x 200 g (7 oz) monkfish tails, skinned
pepper
2 large slices Parma ham
8 basil leaves
2 tablespoons extra virgin olive oil
salt and pepper

1 quantity Olive Oil and Garlic Mash (see page 107)

Preheat the oven to 200°C/400°F/Gas Mark 6. Put the balsamic vinegar into a saucepan and heat gently until boiling. Simmer over a medium heat for 30 minutes or until the vinegar is reduced to about 150ml/$\frac{1}{4}$ pint and is thick and syrupy. You will need to watch closely, especially during the final 5 minutes, as the sauce can over-reduce to a sticky mass. Set aside to cool completely and store in a screw top jar or bottle.

Season the monkfish with pepper. Lay the Parma ham slices flat on a chopping board and arrange 4 basil leaves down each slice. Place the monkfish fillets on top and roll up the ham to enclose the fish. Secure with cocktail sticks.

Heat the oil in a frying pan and fry the monkfish over a medium heat for 3 minutes until evenly browned. Transfer to a baking tray and bake for 7–8 minutes. Remove the fish from the oven, rest for 3 minutes and serve with Olive Oil and Garlic Mash and a good drizzle of the balsamic glaze.

SWORDFISH WITH CANNELLINI BEAN MASH

Serves: 4
Preparation time: 15 minutes
Cooking time: 15 minutes

Tuna can be used instead of swordfish in this dish.

2 tbsp extra virgin olive oil, plus extra for brushing
1 small onion, finely chopped
1 garlic cloves, crushed
1 tsp chopped fresh rosemary
1 x 400 g (13 oz) can of cannellini beans, drained
grated zest and juice of $\frac{1}{2}$ unwaxed lemon
2 tbsp water
salt and pepper
2 x 200 g (7 oz) swordfish steaks

Heat the oil in a frying pan and gently fry the onion, garlic and rosemary over a low heat for 10 minutes until the onion is softened. Stir in the beans, lemon zest and juice, water and salt and pepper. Cover and simmer for 5 minutes. Using a potato masher, mash the bean mixture until fairly smooth and keep warm.

Heat a ridged grill pan or heavy-based frying pan until hot, brush the swordfish steaks with the oil, season with salt and pepper and cook for $1\frac{1}{2}$ minutes each side until cooked through. Rest for 3 minutes.

Arrange the bean mash and swordfish on plates and drizzle over a little extra oil. Serve at once.

BEER-BATTERED FISH WITH OVEN CHIPS

Serves: 2
Preparation time: 10 minutes
Cooking time: 40–45 minutes

When deep-frying food always use a deep, heavy-based saucepan, don't use more than about 5 cm/2 in of oil and, if possible, use a sugar thermometer so you can accurately measure the temperature.

> 500 g (1 lb) main crop potatoes, such as Desiree or King Edwards
> 2 tbsp sunflower oil, plus extra for deep frying
> salt and pepper
> 1 egg, separated
> 100 ml (3^1/$_2$ fl oz) light beer
> 75 g (3 oz) plain flour, plus extra for dusting
> 2 x 200 g (7 oz) skinless cod or haddock fillets
>
> tomato ketchup, to serve

Preheat the oven to 220°C/425°F/Gas Mark 7. Boil the potatoes for 10 minutes, drain, refresh under cold water and pat dry. Cut the potatoes into thick wedges, place in a small roasting tin and toss with half the oil and some salt and pepper. Roast for 40–45 minutes until golden and tender, turning half way through. Keep warm.

Whisk together the remaining oil, egg yolk, beer, flour and salt and pepper. Set aside for 30 minutes. Whisk the egg white until stiff and gently fold into the batter. Heat 5 cm/2 in sunflower in a deep, heavy-based saucepan until reaches 180°C/350°F on a sugar thermometer (or until a cube of bread crisps in 30 seconds).

Dip the fish fillets into the batter, making sure they are totally covered. Using metal tongs, carefully slip a fillet into the hot oil and deep-fry one at a time for 6 minutes until crisp and golden.

Drain the fish on kitchen paper and serve at once with the oven-roasted chips and tomato ketchup.

PAN-FRIED SQUID WITH GARLIC AND LEMON

Serves: 2
Preparation time: 10 minutes
Cooking time: 3–4 minutes

500 g (1 lb) prepared squid tubes
4 tbsp extra virgin olive oil
salt and pepper
2 garlic cloves, crushed
1 tbsp chopped fresh parsley
juice of $\frac{1}{2}$ lemon

olive oil, for spraying

To serve:
green salad
crusty bread

Cut the squid tubes in half, turn over and lay flat so the inside of the tube faces upwards. Using a sharp knife, score a diamond pattern across the squid and then cut each piece into quarters. Toss with half the oil and salt and pepper to taste.

Combine the remaining oil, garlic, parsley and lemon juice in a bowl.

Heat a frying pan or ridged grill pan, spray lightly with olive oil and fry the squid for $1\frac{1}{2}$–2 minutes until lightly golden.

Transfer the squid to a warmed platter and pour over the garlic and lemon oil. Serve hot with a green salad and bread to mop up the delicious juices.

STIR-FRIED FISH WITH GINGER
AND SWEET CHILLI

Serves 2
Preparation time: 20 minutes
Cooking time: 6 minutes

350 g (12 oz) skinless white fish fillets, such as cod or
haddock
1 tsp salt
3 tbsp sunflower oil
2.5 cm (1 in) piece of root ginger, shredded
2 garlic cloves, chopped
100 g ($3^1/_2$ oz) broccoli, trimmed
100 g ($3^1/_2$ oz) mangetout, trimmed
4 spring onions, thickly sliced
100 ml ($3^1/_2$ fl oz) fish stock
1 tbsp Thai fish sauce
1 tbsp dark soy sauce
1 tbsp sweet chilli sauce

cooked rice or noodles, to serve

Cut the fish into 2.5 cm/1 in chunks, rub all over with the salt and
set aside while preparing the remaining ingredients. Wash the fish and
dry thoroughly on kitchen paper.

Heat 2 tablespoons of the oil in a wok until smoking, add the fish and
stir-fry for 2–3 minutes until golden all over. Remove with a slotted spoon.

Add the remaining oil to the wok, add the broccoli, mange tout and
spring onions and stir-fry for 2 minutes. Return the fish to the pan and
add the stock, fish sauce, soy sauce and sweet chilli sauce. Cook for a
further 1 minute and serve with rice or noodles.

ROASTED COD WITH GARLIC
AND PARSLEY OIL

Serves: 4
Preparation time: 5 minutes
Cooking time: 10 minutes

You will need either an ovenproof frying pan or a heavy-based roasting tin for this dish as it is used both on top of the stove and in the oven.

1 tbsp extra virgin olive oil
15 g ($^{1}/_{2}$ oz) butter
2 x 200 g (7 oz) cod fillets
salt and pepper
$^{1}/_{2}$ bunch flat leaf parsley
1 garlic clove, crushed
150 ml ($^{1}/_{4}$ pint) olive oil

mashed potato and steamed green beans, to serve

Preheat the oven to 200°C/400°F/Gas Mark 6. Heat the oil and butter in an ovenproof frying pan or heavy-based roasting tin until the butter stops foaming. Season the cod fillets and fry, skin-side down, for 2 minutes. Turn the cod over and transfer to the oven. Roast for 8–10 minutes until cooked through. Remove from the oven and rest for 5 minutes.

Put the parsley, garlic, oil and a little salt and pepper into a food processor and process until really smooth. Adjust seasonings and serve the cod drizzled with the oil, and mash and steamed green beans.

BAKED COD WITH TOMATOES AND MARJORAM

Serves: 2
Preparation time: 15 minutes
Cooking time: 15 minutes

2 x 200 g (7 oz) cod or haddock fillets
salt and pepper
125 g (4 oz) cherry tomatoes, halved
2 anchovy fillets, diced
50 g (2 oz) pitted black olives
1 tbsp capers in brine, drained
2 sprigs fresh marjoram
2 tbsp extra virgin olive oil
1 tbsp lemon juice

tin foil, to make parcels
Olive Oil and Garlic Mash (see page 107) to serve

Preheat the oven to 200°C/400°F/Gas Mark 6. Season the fish fillets on both sides with salt and pepper and place each one on a large square of tin foil. Pull the edges of the foil up slightly to form a 'bowl' and top the fish with the tomatoes, anchovies, olives, capers and a sprig of marjoram.

Drizzle each fish with oil and lemon juice, bring the edges of the foil up and fold over to seal in the fish and vegetables. Place the parcels on a baking tray and bake for 15 minutes. Remove from the oven, rest for 5 minutes and serve hot with Olive Oil and Garlic Mash.

CORIANDER AND LIME PRAWNS WITH SESAME RICE

Serves: 2
Preparation time: 20 minutes
Cooking time: 6 minutes

Jasmine rice used in Thai cooking and has a wonderfully fragrant flavour. Long-grain rice can be used instead. To cook the sesame seeds, heat a small frying pan, and toast the seeds until they are golden brown.

500 g (1 lb) large raw tiger prawns
$1/2$ bunch fresh coriander, roots attached
1 tsp black peppercorns, ground
$1/2$ tsp salt
1 garlic clove, crushed
2 Kaffir lime leaves, torn
3 tbsp extra virgin olive oil
juice of 1 lime

Sesame rice:
200 g (7 oz) jasmine rice
400 ml (14 fl oz) water
2 tsp salt
2 tsp sesame seeds, toasted
2 tsp sesame oil

bamboo skewers soaked for 30 minutes

Peel the prawns, leaving the tail section intact. Cut a shallow slit along the back of each prawn and pull out and discard the black intestinal tract. Wash and dry the prawns and place in a bowl.

Place the coriander leaves and roots (scrubbed first), peppercorns, salt, garlic, lime leaves and oil in a food processor and process until smooth. Pour over the prawns, stir well until evenly coated and marinate for 30 minutes.

Place the rice in a saucepan with the water and salt, bring to the boil, cover and simmer gently for 10 minutes. Turn off the heat but leave undisturbed for a further 10 minutes. Stir in the sesame seeds and oil.

Preheat the grill to high. Thread the prawns on to the soaked bamboo skewers and grill for 3–4 minutes, turning half way through until cooked. Squeeze over the lime juice and serve with the sesame rice.

AVOCADO AND PRAWN COUSCOUS WITH LIME DRESSING

Serves: 2
Preparation time: 15 minutes, plus soaking

125 g (4 oz) couscous
150 ml ($\frac{1}{2}$ pint) warm water
2 spring onions, trimmed and chopped
1 ripe tomato, chopped
2 tbsp chopped fresh coriander
2 tbsp chopped fresh mint
12 large cooked prawns, peeled, de-veined and halved
1 small avocado, peeled, stoned and diced

Lime dressing:
grated zest and juice of 1 lime
1 tsp clear honey
3 tbsp extra virgin olive oil
salt and pepper

Place the couscous in a bowl and pour over the water. Stir well and leave to soak for 15 minutes or until the grains are swollen. Fluff up the couscous with a fork and stir in the onions, tomato, coriander, mint, prawns and avocado.

Make the dressing: whisk the ingredients together, pour over the couscous mixture and toss well. Adjust seasonings and serve.

INDIAN SPICED PRAWNS WITH MUSTARD SEEDS

Serves: 2
Preparation time: 15 minutes, plus 15 minutes marinating
Cooking time: 8–10 minutes

When frying mustard seeds in hot oil always cover the pan with a lid, as the seeds pop and they will literally jump out of the pan and escape!

350 g (12 oz) large raw tiger prawns, peeled and deveined
   (see page 79)
1 garlic clove, crushed
1 tsp grated root ginger
$1/2$ tsp ground turmeric
$1/2$ tsp garam masala
2 tbsp sunflower oil
salt and pepper
2 tsp mustard seeds
2 large ripe tomatoes, finely chopped
100 ml ($3^1/2$ fl oz) water
50 g (2 oz) Greek-style yogurt
2 tbsp chopped fresh coriander

plain boiled basmati rice, to serve

Place the prawns in a bowl and add the garlic, ginger, spices, $1/2$ tablespoon of the oil and a little salt and pepper. Stir well to coat the prawns and marinate for 15 minutes.

Heat the remaining oil in a wok or frying pan, add the prawns and stir-fry for 2–3 minutes until lightly golden. Remove with a slotted spoon and set aside. Add the mustard seeds to the pan, cover with a lid and heat for 1 minute. Add the tomatoes and water and simmer gently, covered, for 5 minutes. Add the prawns, yogurt and coriander and heat through for 1 minute without boiling. Season to taste and serve with plain basmati rice.

CHAR-GRILLED SALMON WITH ALMOND AND PARSLEY PESTO

Serves: 2
Preparation time: 15 minutes, plus cooling
Cooking time: 10–12 minutes

Use any leftover pesto as a sandwich filling with tomatoes and canned tuna.

2 x 200 g (7 oz) salmon fillets
1 tbsp extra virgin olive oil, plus extra for drizzling
1 lime, halved

Almond and parsley pesto:
25 g (1 oz) blanched almonds
1 garlic clove, crushed
$\frac{1}{2}$ bunch flat leaf parsley
1 tbsp capers in brine, drained
2 tbsp grated Parmesan cheese
salt and pepper
60 ml ($2\frac{1}{2}$ fl oz) extra virgin olive oil

Make the pesto: heat a frying pan, add the almonds and fry for 3–4 minutes until charred. Leave to cool and then transfer to a food processor. Add the garlic, parsley leaves, capers, Parmesan and salt and pepper and process briefly until finely chopped. Add the oil and process again to form a fairly smooth paste. Adjust seasoning and set aside until required.

Heat a ridged grill pan until hot. Season the salmon with salt and pepper, brush with oil and char-grill for 3–4 minutes each side. Transfer the salmon to serving plates, top with a spoonful of the pesto, squeeze over the lime juice and serve drizzled with a little extra oil.

SALMON STEAK BAGUETTE WITH TAPENADE

Serves: 2
Preparation time: 15 minutes
Cooking time: 17 minutes

You will need either $^1/_2$ a large baguette or 1 medium baguette for this dish.

> 200 g (7 oz) salmon fillet, skinned
> salt and pepper
> 2 tbsp olive oil
> 1 red onion, sliced thinly
> a pinch of sugar
> 1 tsp chopped fresh thyme
> 1 medium baguette
> 2 tbsp tapenade (olive paste)
> a few wild rocket leaves
> $^1/_2$ lemon

Slice the salmon into 5 mm/$^1/_4$in thick slices and season with salt and pepper.

Heat half the oil in a heavy-based frying pan and fry the onions, sugar, a pinch of salt and the thyme for 15 minutes until the onion is golden and caramelised. Transfer the onions to a bowl and wipe the frying pan clean. Heat the remaining oil and fry the salmon, in batches, for 1 minute on each side until golden.

Slice almost through the baguette and spread with the olive paste. Fill with rocket, the onions and the salmon pieces. Squeeze over the lemon juice, cut the baguette in half and serve at once.

TERIYAKI SALMON WITH MANGETOUT

Serves: 2
Preparation time: 5 minutes, plus marinating
Cooking: 20 minutes

Sake and mirin are both made from rice and are used extensively in Japanese cooking, Both are available from healthfood stores and some larger supermarkets.

50 ml (2 fl oz) dark soy sauce
50 ml (2 fl oz) sake (Japanese rice wine)
2 tbsp mirin (sweetened rice wine)
1 tbsp caster sugar
2 x 200 g (7 oz) salmon fillets
15 g ($1/2$ oz) butter
175 g (6 oz) mangetout, trimmed
$1/2$ tbsp light soy sauce
1 tsp sesame oil

boiled rice, to serve

Mix the soy sauce, sake, mirin and sugar together and stir until the sugar is dissolved. Pour over the salmon and marinate for 10 minutes.

Preheat the grill to high. Remove the salmon from its marinade and grill for 3 minutes, then turn and cook for a further 3–4 minutes until lightly charred and cooked through. Transfer the salmon to warmed plates and cover loosely with foil. Rest for 3 minutes.

Pour the marinade juices into a saucepan and bring to the boil. Simmer for 2 minutes until thickened and gradually whisk in the butter until the sauce is glossy.

Cook the mangetout in a saucepan of lightly salted boiling water for 3 minutes. Drain well, return to the pan and add the light soy sauce and sesame oil.

Spoon the sauce over the salmon and serve with the mangetout and boiled rice.

MUSSELS WITH COCONUT, CHILLI AND SESAME BROTH

Serves: 2
Preparation time: 15 minutes
Cooking time: 5 minutes

1 kg (2 lb) fresh mussels
1 large red chilli, deseeded and sliced
1 stalk lemongrass, roughly chopped
4 Kaffir lime leaves, torn
2 garlic cloves, chopped
$\frac{1}{2}$ bunch of fresh coriander, roughly torn
200 ml (7 fl oz) coconut milk
juice of 2 limes
2 tsp sesame oil

Scrub the mussels in cold water and pull off the scraggly 'beard' that may still be attached to the shell. Shake dry and place the mussels in a large saucepan with the remaining ingredients. Bring to the boil, cover and simmer for 4–5 minutes, shaking the pan occasionally, until all the mussels have opened (discard any that remain closed).

Divide the mussels between warmed serving bowls and strain over the juice. Serve hot.

MUSSELS AND PASTA MARINARA

Serves: 2
Preparation time: 15 minutes
Cooking time: 15 minutes

Farmed mussels are available year-round and are really good quality. They are far quicker and easier to prepare than wild mussels as they tend to be cleaner.

2 tbsp extra virgin olive oil
2 garlic cloves, chopped
a pinch of dried red chilli flakes
100 ml (3$\frac{1}{2}$ fl oz) white wine
1 x 400 g (13 oz) can chopped tomatoes
2 tbsp chopped fresh parsley
1 kg (2 lb) fresh mussels, scrubbed
pepper
225 g (8 oz) dried tagliatelle

Heat the oil in a saucepan and gently fry the garlic and chilli for 2–3 minutes over a low heat. Add the wine and cook for 1 minute. Add the tomatoes, parsley, mussels and a little pepper. Bring to the boil, cover and simmer gently for 4–5 minutes until all the mussels have opened. Discard any that remain closed.

Strain the sauce and return to the pan (reserving the mussels). Bring to the boil and simmer over a medium heat for 5 minutes until reduced and thickened slightly. Return the mussels to the pan and warm through.

Plunge the pasta into a saucepan of lightly salted, boiling water and cook according to the packet instructions until al dente. Drain well and divide between warmed serving bowls. Add the mussels and sauce and serve hot.

SEAFOOD PIZZA

Serves: 2
Preparation time: 15 minutes
Cooking time: 18 minutes

1 x quantity basic pizza dough (see page 21)
12 large raw peeled tiger prawns
2 tbsp extra virgin olive oil
2 garlic cloves, sliced
200 g (7 oz) prepared squid tubes, sliced into rings
3 tbsp sun-dried tomato paste
200 g (7 oz) can tuna in oil, drained
a pinch of dried oregano
1 tbsp drained capers
200 g (7 oz) mozzarella, diced
salt and pepper

flour, for dusting

Make up the pizza dough according to the recipe on page 21.

Preheat the oven to 230°C/450°F/Gas Mark 8 and put two baking trays into the oven to heat up. Devein the prawns if necessary, wash and pat dry. Heat the oil in a frying pan and gently fry the prawns, garlic and squid for 1–2 minutes until just cooked. Remove to a plate.

Knock back the risen pizza dough, divide in half and roll out each piece on a lightly floured surface and use to line two 23 cm/9 in shallow cake tins.

Spread each pizza base with sun-dried tomato paste and top with the cooked seafood, tuna, oregano, capers, mozzarella and salt and pepper. Bake on the heated baking trays for 10–15 minutes until the cheese is bubbling and golden. Serve hot.

VEGETABLES

You can make any of the vegetable dishes below from your weekly shop and your basic store cupboard. Most of the fresh ingredients are highlighted in the fridge. Any extra seasonings and side dishes to serve are listed here.

POTATOES
FRESH ROSEMARY
FRESH ROOT GINGER
CANNED BORLOTTI BEANS
CANNED SWEETCORN KERNELS
RED LENTILS
FROZEN BROAD BEANS
FROZEN PEAS
CRUSTY BREAD
SOUR DOUGH BREAD
BURGER BUNS
DOLCELATTE CHEESE
FONTINA CHEESE
TOFU
KAFFIR LIME LEAVES
DRIED OREGANO
SZECHUAN PEPPERCORNS
CHINESE FIVE-SPICE POWDER
DRIED RED CHILLI FLAKES
CURRY POWDER
BASIL PESTO
THAI SWEET CHILLI SAUCE
SWEET SOY SAUCE
WALNUT OIL
SESAME OIL
MANGO CHUTNEY
REDCURRANT JELLY
CLEAR HONEY
DRY WHITE WINE
SHERRY
FAST-ACTING YEAST
PECAN NUTS
WALNUTS
OLIVE TAPENADE
BLACK OLIVES
ANCHOVIES IN OIL

TUSCAN BEAN SOUP

Serves: 2
Preparation time: 10 minutes
Cooking time: 30 minutes

2 tbsp extra virgin olive oil
1 small onion, chopped
1 garlic clove, chopped
1 tsp chopped fresh rosemary
250 g (8 oz) ripe tomatoes, roughly chopped
1 x 400 g (13 oz) can borlotti beans, drained
600 ml (1 pint) vegetable stock.
salt and pepper
50 g (2 oz) baby spinach leaves
1 tbsp chopped fresh parsley

To serve:
freshly grated Parmesan
crusty bread

Heat the oil in a saucepan and gently fry the onion, garlic and rosemary for 5 minutes until softened. Add the tomatoes, beans, vegetable stock and salt and pepper to taste.

Bring to the boil and simmer gently, covered, for 20 minutes. Stir in the spinach leaves and parsley and cook for a further 5 minutes. Transfer half the soup to a liquidizer and blend until smooth. Return to the pan and warm through.

Spoon the soup into warmed bowls, top with grated Parmesan and serve with crusty bread.

CARROT SOUP WITH CORIANDER AND LIME BUTTER

Serves: 4
Preparation time: 10 minutes
Cooking time: 25 minutes

This recipe makes enough for 4 servings, but soup keeps well in the fridge for up to 2 days or it can be frozen for up to 1 month.

1 onion, chopped
1 garlic clove, crushed
750 g (1 $^1/_2$ lb) carrots, chopped
1 litre (1 $^3/_4$ pints) vegetable stock

Coriander and lime butter:
125 g (4 oz) butter, softened
grated zest of 1 lime
juice of $^1/_2$ lime
1 tbsp chopped fresh coriander
salt and pepper

crusty bread, to serve

Make the butter: beat the butter, lime zest and juice, coriander and a little salt and pepper together until smooth. Place in a small square of foil, roll into a log, wrap in the foil and chill until required.

Put the onion, garlic, carrots, stock in a saucepan, salt and pepper to taste and bring to the boil. Cover and simmer gently for 25 minutes until the carrots are cooked.

Transfer to a liquidizer and blend until really smooth. Return to the pan, adjust seasoning and heat through. Cut the butter into thin slices.

Spoon the soup into bowls, top each with 2 slices of the butter and serve with crusty bread.

THAI CORN CAKES

Serves: 2 (makes 10 cakes)
Preparation time: 10 minutes
Cooking time: 5 minutes

Kaffir lime leaves with their wonderful fragrance and flavour are used extensively in South East Asian cooking. They are available from larger supermarkets, Asian food stores and some specialist greengrocers. To prepare the lime leaves, separate the leaves and cut away the thick central stalk.

65 g (2½ oz) plain flour
½ tsp baking powder
1 egg, lightly beaten
1½ tbsp light soy sauce
1 tbsp lime juice
150 g (5 oz) canned sweetcorn kernels, drained
4 Kaffir lime leaves, very finely shredded
1 tbsp chopped fresh coriander

vegetable oil, for frying
sweet chilli sauce, to serve

Sift the flour and baking powder into a food processor. Add the egg, soy sauce, lime juice, half the sweetcorn, lime leaves and coriander and process to a thick purée. Transfer the mixture to a bowl and stir in the remaining sweetcorn.

Heat a shallow layer of oil in a frying pan, then drop in heaped tablespoons of batter, four at a time, pressing to flatten into small cakes. Fry for 1–1½ minutes each side until cooked through. Drain on kitchen paper and repeat until you have 10 cakes. Serve hot with some sweet chilli sauce, to dip.

VEGETABLE AND LENTIL CURRY

Serves 4
Preparation time: 20 minutes
Cooking time: 40–45 minutes

You can use a hot curry powder instead, if you wish, depending on your tolerance of chilli.

3 tbsp vegetable oil
1 onion, sliced
1 garlic clove, chopped
1 tsp grated root ginger
1 tbsp medium curry powder
1 tsp ground cinnamon
150 g (5 oz) potato, peeled and cubed
1 x 400 g (13 oz) can chopped tomatoes
450 ml ($^3/_4$ pint) vegetable stock
salt and pepper
50 g (2 oz) red lentils
125 g (4 oz) button mushrooms, halved
125 g (4 oz) frozen peas
125 g (4 oz) cauliflower florets, diced
1 tbsp chopped fresh coriander

To serve:
plain boiled basmati rice
raita (see page 20)
mango chutney

Heat the oil in a saucepan and fry the onion, garlic, ginger, curry powder and cinnamon for 10 minutes until the onion is softened. Add the potatoes, tomatoes, stock, salt and pepper and lentils. Bring to the boil, cover and simmer gently for 15 minutes.

Add the mushrooms, peas, cauliflower and coriander to the pan and cook for a further 10–15 minutes until all the vegetables are tender. Adjust seasoning and serve with basmati rice, raita and mango chutney.

GRILLED ASPARAGUS, TAPENADE AND HALLOUMI SALAD

Serves: 2
Preparation time: 5 minutes
Cooking time: 5 minutes

Although asparagus is available year-round it is always best during the early summer months – between late May and the end of June. Halloumi is a ewe's milk cheese from Cyprus. It has a distinctive sharp/salty flavour and is always served cooked. It is available from most supermarkets or continental food shops.

500 g (1 lb) asparagus spears
1 tbsp extra virgin olive oil
125 g (4 oz) halloumi, sliced thinly
a handful of rocket leaves

Tapenade dressing:
1 tbsp olive tapenade
3 tbsp extra virgin olive oil
1 tbsp lemon juice
2 tsp honey
salt and pepper

Make the dressing: place all the ingredients in a screwtop jar and shake until evenly blended. Season to taste and set aside until required.

Trim the thick ends of the asparagus spears and place the spears on a baking tray. Add a little oil and some salt and pepper and roll the asparagus until it is coated evenly.

Heat a ridged grill pan or conventional grill until hot and cook the asparagus for 4–5 minutes, turning half way through, until it is charred and tender. Transfer the asparagus to a large platter.

Heat a heavy-based frying pan until hot, add the halloumi slices and fry for 1 minute on each side until browned and softened. Arrange over the asparagus, top with the rocket leaves and serve drizzled with the tapenade dressing.

MUSHROOM AND HALLOUMI BURGER WITH ONION JAM

Serves: 2
Preparation time: 15 minutes
Cooking time: 40 minutes

2 large flat mushrooms
salt and pepper
2 tbsp extra virgin olive oil
125 g (4 oz) halloumi cheese, thinly sliced
2 burger buns, halved
a little shredded lettuce
soured cream, optional

Onion jam:
2 tbsp extra virgin olive oil
2 onions, thinly sliced
75 g (3 oz) redcurrant jelly
1 tbsp red wine vinegar
2 tbsp water
salt and pepper

Make the onion jam: heat the oil in a saucepan and fry the onion for 15–20 minutes until caramelized, add the remaining ingredients and continue to cook for a further 5–10 minutes until jam-like. Leave to go cold.

Trim the stalks from the mushrooms and season lightly with salt and pepper. Heat the oil in a large frying pan and fry the mushrooms for 6–8 minutes each side until tender, remove from the pan and keep warm. Wipe the pan clean and return to the heat.

Add the halloumi to the frying pan and cook for 1 minute each side until golden and softened slightly.

Toast the burger buns. Fill the buns with shredded lettuce leaves, the mushrooms, halloumi, onion jam and a little soured cream, if using.

ROCKET, PEAR AND PARMESAN SALAD WITH WALNUT OIL

Serves: 2
Preparation time: 5 minutes

Walnut oil adds a lovely nutty flavour to salad dressings and is readily available from many supermarkets or delis. Buy a small quantity and store in the fridge once opened as this lengthens the oil's shelf life.

100 g (3^1/$_2$ oz) wild rocket leaves
1 ripe pear, quartered, cored and thinly sliced
50 g (2 oz) Parmesan cheese, shaved or grated
25 g (1 oz) walnuts, toasted and finely chopped

Walnut dressing:
2 tbsp walnut oil
1 tbsp extra virgin olive oil
2 tsp sherry or balsamic vinegar
^{1}/$_2$ tsp caster sugar
salt and pepper

Combine the rocket, pear, Parmesan and walnuts in a bowl.
Place the dressing ingredients in a screwtop jar and shake until blended. Pour over the salad and serve immediately.

FOUR CHEESE AND TOMATO PIZZA

Serves: 2
Preparation time: 10 minutes
Cooking time: 8–10 minutes

Unless you have a pizza stone, it is best to cook these pizzas in shallow cake tins. I find the bases of my spring-form cake tins are ideal or you can buy pizza trays from cookware shops.

2 ripe plum tomatoes, seeded and diced
$1/2$ tbsp extra virgin olive oil
2 tsp dried oregano
salt and pepper
50 g (2 oz) Fontina cheese, diced
50 g (2 oz) mozzarella, diced
50 g (2 oz) Dolcelatte, crumbled
25 g (1 oz) freshly grated Parmesan cheese

Basic pizza dough:
250 g (8 oz) plain flour
$1/2$ tsp salt
$1 1/2$ tsp fast-acting yeast
125 ml (4 fl oz) warm water
1 tbsp extra virgin olive oil

flour, for dusting

Make the pizza dough: sift the flour and salt into a bowl, stir in the yeast and make a well in the middle. Gradually work in the water and oil to form a soft dough, transfer to a lightly floured surface and knead the dough for 8–10 minutes until smooth and elastic. Shape into a ball and place in an oiled bowl, cover with cling film and leave the dough to rise in a warm place for 45 minutes or until doubled in size.

Divide the dough in half, roll each half out on a lightly floured surface, then use to line two 23 cm/9 in shallow cake tins.

Preheat the oven to 230°C/450°F/Gas mark 8 and place a large baking tray on the middle shelf to heat up.

Combine the tomatoes, oil, oregano and salt and pepper in a bowl and scatter over the pizza bases. Top with the four cheeses and bake on the heated baking tray for 10–12 minutes until bubbling and golden. Serve hot.

RISOTTO WITH BEANS, PEAS AND BACON

Serves: 2
Preparation time: 25 minutes
Cooking time: 30–35 minutes

If you don't have time to make your own, fresh chicken stock is available from larger supermarkets or butchers. It tends to have a more natural flavour than stock cubes, which should be used as a last resort.

600–750 ml (1–1$\frac{1}{4}$ pints) fresh chicken stock
2 tbsp extra virgin olive oil
75 g (3 oz) piece smoked bacon, diced
1 onion, finely chopped
1 garlic clove, crushed
150 g (5 oz) arborio (risotto) rice
75 ml (3 fl oz) dry white wine
125 g (4 oz) frozen broad beans
100 g (3$\frac{1}{2}$ oz) frozen peas
salt and pepper
2 tbsp basil pesto

freshly grated Parmesan, to serve

Put the stock into a saucepan and bring to a very gentle simmer.

Heat the oil in a saucepan and fry the bacon, onion and garlic for 5 minutes until softened. Add the rice, stir-fry for 30 seconds until the grains are glossy and add the wine. Boil for 1–2 minutes until the wine is absorbed and then add the beans, peas and salt and pepper to taste.

Pour in a ladleful of the simmering stock and bring to the boil. Cook, stirring constantly, for 3–4 minutes until the stock is absorbed. Continue adding the stock a ladleful at a time and stirring the rice for 20–25 minutes until the rice is tender and all the stock absorbed.

Remove the pan from the heat, stir in the pesto, cover and rest for 5 minutes. Serve with freshly grated Parmesan.

PASTA WITH CHERRY TOMATO SAUCE

Serves: 2
Preparation time: 15 minutes
Cooking time: 15 minutes

250 g (8 oz) dried pasta
4 tbsp extra virgin olive oil
1 garlic clove, sliced
a pinch dried red chilli flakes
salt and pepper
250 g (8 oz) cherry tomatoes, halved
75 g (3 oz) pitted black olives, halved
4 anchovies in oil, drained and chopped
2 tbsp baby capers in brine, drained and washed
2 tbsp chopped fresh basil

freshly grated Parmesan, to serve
basil leaves, to garnish

Plunge the pasta into a saucepan of lightly salted, boiling water and cook according to packet instructions. Drain well, reserving 4 tablespoons of the cooking water and return pasta to the pan.

Heat the oil in a large frying pan and gently fry the garlic, chilli and some salt and pepper for 5 minutes until softened. Add the tomatoes, stir-fry for 1 minute and then stir in the olives, anchovies, capers and basil.

Heat gently for 3–4 minutes and then stir in the cooked pasta and reserved cooking water. Stir over a low heat for 1–2 minutes, transfer to serving bowls and top with some grated Parmesan. Garnish with the basil leaves.

COURGETTE AND LEMON PASTA

Serves: 2
Preparation time: 15 minutes
Cooking time: 15 minutes

Pecorino is a Sardinian ewe's milk cheese with a delightfully nutty, almost sweet flavour. It is a hard cheese similar to Parmesan, which can be substituted if wished. The heat from the pasta is sufficient to cook the grated courgette.

2 courgettes
250 g (8 oz) dried spaghetti
4 tbsp extra virgin olive oil
2 garlic cloves, finely chopped
grated zest and juice of 1 lemon
1/2 bunch of fresh mint leaves, torn
25 g (1 oz) freshly grated Pecorino or Parmesan cheese

extra virgin olive oil, to serve

Grate the courgettes coarsely using a box grater. Place in the middle of a clean tea towel, wrap and squeeze out as much liquid as possible.

Plunge the pasta into a pan of lightly salted, boiling water and cook according to the packet instructions. Drain well, reserving 4 tablespoons of the cooking water.

Heat the oil in a large frying pan and gently fry the garlic, lemon zest and salt and pepper to taste for 2–3 minutes until the garlic is soft but not browned. Add the cooked pasta, courgettes, reserved cooking water, lemon juice, mint and half the Pecorino and stir well until the pasta is evenly coated.

Spoon the pasta into bowls, top with the remaining cheese and serve drizzled with a little more olive oil.

BRUSCHETTA WITH BUTTERNUT SQUASH AND GOAT'S CHEESE

Serves: 2
Preparation time: 10 minutes
Cooking time: 15–20 minutes

Feta can be used instead of the goat's cheese, if preferred.

> 500 g (1lb) butternut squash, peeled and diced (about
>   350 g/12 oz prepared weight)
> 3 tbsp extra virgin olive oil, plus extra to drizzle
> 1 sprig fresh rosemary, leaves only
> salt and pepper
> 2 large slices sourdough bread
> 2 tbsp olive tapenade
> 50 g (2 oz) goat's cheese, crumbled
> a few baby rocket leaves
> 2 tsp balsamic vinegar

Preheat the oven to 220°C/425°F/Gas Mark 7. Put the squash into a roasting tin with 1 tablespoon of oil, the rosemary leaves and salt and pepper and roast for 15–20 minutes until soft and lightly browned. Remove from the oven.

Char-grill the bread slices on a heated ridged grill pan (or toast under a grill) and spread each one with the tapenade. Top with the squash, goat's cheese and some rocket leaves.

Whisk the remaining oil, balsamic vinegar and salt and pepper together, drizzle over the bruschetta and serve at once.

PENNE WITH LEEKS, BACON AND DOLCELATTE

Serves: 2
Preparation time: 10 minutes
Cooking time: 11 minutes

250 g (8 oz) dried penne
2 tbsp extra virgin olive oil
2 rashers smoked back bacon, diced
1 large leek, trimmed and sliced
1 garlic clove, crushed
50 ml (2 fl oz) single cream
100 g (3$\frac{1}{2}$ oz) Dolcelatte
50 g (2 oz) pecan nuts, toasted and finely chopped
salt and pepper

freshly grated Parmesan, to serve

Plunge the pasta into a saucepan of lightly salted, boiling water and cook according to the packet instructions until al dente. Drain well and return the cooked pasta to the pan.

Heat the oil in a frying pan, add the bacon and fry for 3 minutes until golden, then remove with a slotted spoon. Add the leeks and garlic to the pan and fry for 6–8 minutes until softened. Stir in the pasta, bacon, cream, Dolcelatte and pecan nuts and heat gently, stirring over a low heat for 1 minute or until the cheese is melted.

Season to taste, transfer the pasta to warmed bowls and serve topped with grated Parmesan.

SALT AND SPICE SWEETCORN

Serves: 2
Preparation time: 5 minutes
Cooking time: 10 minutes

2 heads sweetcorn, trimmed and peeled
50 g (2 oz) unsalted butter, softened
1/2 tsp ground Szechuan peppercorns (see page 53)
1/2 tsp sea salt
1/4 tsp Chinese five-spice powder

Cook the sweetcorn in a large pot of lightly salted, boiling water for 10 minutes until tender. Drain well and transfer to serving plates.

Place the butter, Szechuan pepper, salt and Chinese five-spice powder in a small saucepan and heat gently until melted. Drizzle over the sweetcorn and serve hot.

OLIVE OIL AND GARLIC MASH

Serves: 2
Prep time: 5 minutes
Cooking time: 12–15 minutes

Main crop potatoes vary considerably in texture as well as flavour. Look for those labelled floury or suitable for mashing such as King Edward or Desiree.

500 g (1 lb) main crop potatoes, cut into chunks
3 large garlic cloves, roughly chopped
50 ml (2 fl oz) extra virgin olive oil
salt and pepper

Place the potatoes and garlic in a large saucepan, and add cold water to cover by at least 5cm/2 in. Season with salt and bring to the boil, then cook for 12–15 minutes until the potatoes are really tender.

Drain the potatoes and garlic well, reserving 2 tablespoons of the cooking water, and return them to the pan. Mash the potatoes and garlic with the reserved water and gradually beat in the oil. Season to taste and serve hot.

SWEET POTATOES WITH BACON, SOURED CREAM AND SWEET CHILLI SAUCE

Serves: 2
Preparation time: 2 minutes
Cooking time: 50 minutes

Sweet potatoes are great baked in their jackets and look stunning with their vivid orange flesh.

> 2 x 200 g (7 oz) sweet potatoes, scrubbed
> 2 rashers smoked back bacon
> 25 g (1 oz) butter
> 50 g (2 oz) soured cream
> 2 tbsp Thai sweet chilli sauce
> salt and pepper

Preheat the oven to 220°C/425°F/Gas Mark 7. Place the potatoes in a roasting tin and roast for about 50 minutes until tender.

Heat a non-stick frying pan until hot, add the bacon and fry for 2–3 minutes until crisp and golden.

Transfer the potatoes to serving plates, cut in half and top each with butter, soured cream, a drizzle of sweet chilli sauce and salt and pepper. Top with the bacon and serve hot.

BARBECUED VEGETABLE SALAD

Serves: 2
Preparation time: 10 minutes
Cooking time: 20 minutes

1 red pepper
1 courgette
1 small aubergine
1 red onion
1 bunch of asparagus spears
1 tbsp extra virgin olive oil
2 tbsp chopped mixed fresh herbs, such as basil, coriander,
    mint and parsley

Dressing:
3 tbsp extra virgin olive oil
1 tbsp red wine vinegar
1 small garlic clove, crushed
salt and pepper

Quarter the pepper, discard the seeds and cut each quarter in half. Cut the courgette and aubergine into thick slices. Cut the onion into wedges and trim the ends from the asparagus spears. Place all the vegetables in a roasting tin and add the oil and salt and pepper to taste. Stir well until evenly coated.

Cook the vegetables on a barbecue or heated ridged grill pan until charred and tender. This will vary from 2–3 minutes for the asparagus and courgettes, 3–4 minutes for the onions and aubergine and 4–5 minutes for the peppers. Transfer all the vegetables to a large bowl.

Whisk the dressing ingredients together and pour over the hot vegetables. Add the herbs, stir well and leave to cool. Serve warm.

BROCCOLI, MARINATED TOFU AND CABBAGE RICE

Serves: 2
Preparation time: 10 minutes
Cooking time: 5 minutes

Tofu is available from the chilled counter in most supermarkets and healthfood stores. Look out for marinated or smoked tofu, which have a better flavour than the plain varieties.

        2 tbsp sunflower oil
        2 tsp sesame oil
        125 g (4 oz) broccoli florets
        1 red pepper, deseeded and diced
        2 garlic cloves, sliced
        125 g (4 oz) Chinese cabbage, shredded
        125 g (4 oz) marinated tofu, diced
        400 g (13 oz) cooked long-grain rice
        2–3 tbsp light soy sauce
        1 tbsp sweet soy sauce
        2 spring onions, thinly sliced

Heat the two oils in a wok or large frying pan, add the broccoli and pepper and stir-fry for 2 minutes. Add the garlic, Chinese cabbage and tofu and stir-fry for 2 minutes. Add the rice and stir-fry for 1 minute.

Add the remaining ingredients and continue to stir-fry for a further 2 minutes until heated through. Serve hot.

FRUIT

The main ingredients that you will need to make any of the following recipes are highlighted in the fridge. Extra ingredients to serve or flavour are shown on the list below.

VANILLA OR CINNAMON ICE CREAM
CLEAR HONEY
MAPLE SYRUP
LEMON CURD
GROUND NUTMEG
GROUND CLOVES
GROUND ALMONDS
GROUND GINGER
GROUND CINNAMON
CRYSTALLISED GINGER
BRIOCHE, PANETTONE OR RAISIN BREAD
WHOLEMEAL BREAD
FILO PASTRY
FROZEN PUFF PASTRY
MUESLI OR GRANOLA
ROLLED OATS
BANANAS
PINE NUTS
HAZELNUTS
PISTACHIO NUTS
RAISINS
ROSEWATER
VEGETABLE OIL SPRAY
CALVADOS OR BRANDY
CRÈME DE CASSIS
SPARKLING APPLE JUICE
DESSERT BISCUITS

GRILLED FIG AND SWEET GOAT CHEESE BRUSCHETTA

Serves: 2
Preparation time: 5 minutes
Cooking time: 3–4 minutes

This may sound a little unusual, but adding some honey to goat's cheese sweetens it, giving the finished dish a lovely flavour and creamy texture. Grilled peaches or nectarines can be used in place of the figs when they are unavailable.

> 6 fresh figs, halved
> 1 tbsp soft brown sugar
> 75 g (3 oz) soft creamy goat's cheese
> 1 tbsp clear honey
> a pinch of ground nutmeg
> 2 slices brioche, panettone or raisin bread

Place the figs on a baking tray and sprinkle over the brown sugar. Cook under a hot grill for 3–4 minutes until softened and lightly charred.

Beat the cheese, honey and nutmeg together until smooth.

Toast the bread (either under the grill or on a preheated ridged grill pan), spread with the goat's cheese mixture and top with the grilled figs. Serve hot.

APPLE FRITTERS WITH ICE CREAM AND CALVADOS

Serves: 2
Preparation time: 5 minutes
Cooking time: 2 minutes

Use a Granny Smith or similar apple for this recipe.

> 1 large eating apple
> 50 g (2 oz) plain flour
> 1/4 tsp bicarbonate of soda
> a pinch of ground cloves
> 1 tsp caster
> 75 ml (3 fl oz) sparkling apple juice
> 2 scoops vanilla ice cream
> 2 tbsp Calvados or brandy
>
> sunflower oil, for deep frying

Quarter and core the apple and then cut each quarter into 3 thin wedges.

Sift the flour, bicarbonate of soda and ground cloves into a bowl, stir in the sugar and then whisk in the sparkling apple juice to form a thick batter with the consistency of thick pouring cream.

Heat 5 cm (2 in) sunflower oil in a deep saucepan until it reaches 180°C/350°F on a sugar thermometer (or until a cube of bread crisps and browns in 30 seconds).

Dip the apple wedges into the batter and then carefully slip them into the hot oil. Fry in batches for 1–2 minutes until crisp and golden. Drain on kitchen paper.

Divide the apple fritters between 2 glasses or bowls, add the ice cream and drizzle with the Calvados or brandy. Serve at once.

YOGURT, MIXED BERRY AND MUESLI COMPOTE

Serves 2
Preparation time: 5 minutes, plus cooling
Cooking time: 2–3 minutes

125 g (4 oz) strawberries, hulled and halved
75 g (3 oz) blackberries or blueberries
75 g (3 oz) raspberries
2 tbsp fresh orange juice
1 tbsp clear honey
250 g (8 oz) Greek-style yogurt
50 g (2 oz) toasted muesli or granola

Put all the berries, orange juice and honey into a saucepan and heat gently for 1–2 minutes until the berries just start to soften. Remove from the heat and leave to cool.

Divide half of the berry mixture between two glasses and top with half the yogurt and half the muesli or granola. Repeat the layers and chill for 30 minutes or serve at once.

EXOTIC FRUIT SALAD WITH MINT AND LIME SUGAR

Serves: 2

Preparation time: 10 minutes, plus chilling

2 tbsp caster sugar
5 g ($^1/_4$ oz) mint leaves, about 12
grated zest and juice of 1 lime
1 mango
$^1/_2$ small pineapple
1 banana
2 ripe passionfruit
juice of 1 orange

Place the sugar, mint leaves and lime zest in a spice grinder or coffee grinder and grind to form a coarse paste.

Peel the mango and cut down each cheek, dice the flesh and place in a bowl. Peel the pineapple and discard the tough central core, dice the flesh and add to the mango. Peel and slice the banana and add to the other fruits.

Sprinkle 2 tablespoons of the mint and lime sugar over the salad. Add the passionfruit pulp, lime juice and orange juice and chill for 15 minutes before serving.

PEAR AND RHUBARB CRUMBLES

Serves: 2
Preparation time: 20 minutes
Cooking time: 25 minutes

250 g (8 oz) rhubarb, chopped (trimmed weight)
175 g (6 oz) pears, cored and chopped
15 g ($^1/_2$ oz) crystallised ginger, finely chopped
50 g (2 oz) caster sugar
2 tbsp water
50 g (2 oz) plain flour
50 g (2 oz) ground almonds
50 g (2 oz) rolled oats
50 g (2 oz) soft brown sugar
1 tsp ground ginger
50 g (2 oz) unsalted butter, finely diced

cream or crème fraîche, to serve

Preheat the oven to 190°C/375°F/Gas Mark 5 and grease two 300 ml ($^1/_2$ pint) baking dishes. Place the rhubarb, pears, crystallised ginger, caster sugar and water into a saucepan and heat gently for 10 minutes until the rhubarb is softened slightly. Transfer to the prepared pie dishes.

Combine the flour, almonds, oats, sugar and ground ginger in a bowl. Add the butter and rub lightly into the mixture. Scatter over the rhubarb mixture and bake for 25 minutes until bubbling and golden. Serve with cream or crème fraîche.

APPLE AND RAISIN STRUDEL

Serves: 2
Preparation time: 20 minutes
Cooking time: 15–20 minutes

Filo pastry is available fresh from the chilled cabinet at most larger supermarkets.

> 1 large eating apple, peeled (about 250 g/8 oz)
> 2 tbsp fresh wholemeal breadcrumbs
> 2 tbsp pine nuts, toasted
> 2 tbsp maple syrup
> 2 tbsp raisins
> 1/4 tsp ground cinnamon
> 4 sheets filo pastry
> 40 g (1 1/2 oz) unsalted butter, melted
> 1 tbsp icing sugar
> 1 tsp ground cinnamon
>
> custard or cream, to serve

Preheat the oven to 190°C/375°F/Gas Mark 5. Quarter and core the apple and cut into small dice. Place in a bowl and add the breadcrumbs, pine nuts, maple syrup, raisins and cinnamon and stir well.

Brush 1 sheet of pastry with melted butter and then top with a second sheet and brush again with butter. Repeat with the remaining pastry.

Cut the pastry in half crossways to form two rectangles and spread half the apple mixture over each one, leaving a 5 cm/2 in border. Fold the long sides over the filling, brush with the melted butter and then fold over from one short side to form a roll.

Transfer to a baking tray, brush with the remaining melted butter and bake for 20 minutes until golden.

Combine the icing sugar and cinnamon and use to dust the strudels. Serve hot with custard or whipped cream.

NECTARINE TARTLETS WITH HAZELNUT BUTTER

Serves: 2
Preparation time: 10 minutes
Cooking time: 20 minutes

1 sheet frozen puff pastry, thawed
50 g (2 oz) unsalted butter, softened
25 g (1 oz) hazelnuts, toasted and finely ground
25 g (1 oz) caster sugar, plus extra for dusting
$1/4$ tsp ground cinnamon
2 nectarines, halved, stoned and quartered

vanilla or cinnamon ice cream, to serve

Preheat the oven to 220°C/425°F/Gas Mark 7. Place the pastry sheet on to a baking tray and, using a sharp knife, score a 1 cm ($1/2$ in) border all the way round the edge, but do not cut completely through the pastry.

Cream the butter, hazelnuts, sugar and cinnamon together until smooth and spread over the pastry up to the edges of the border.

Cut the nectarine quarters into thin slices and arrange in four overlapping lines over the hazelnut butter. Sprinkle with a little extra sugar and bake for 20–25 minutes until the nectarines are cooked and the pastry is golden. Serve hot with vanilla or cinnamon ice cream.

LEMON CURD AND PASSIONFRUIT TARTS

Serves: 2
Preparation time: 30 minutes, plus chilling
Cooking time: 20–25 minutes

When buying passionfruit look for those with a well wrinkled skin; this means that they are ripe and therefore the pulp will be sweet and juicy.

6 passionfruit (about 150 ml/5 fl oz pulp)
50 g (2 oz) caster sugar
50 ml (2 fl oz) water
150 ml (¼ pint) double cream
4 tbsp lemon curd

Sweet shortcrust pastry:
150 g (5 oz) plain flour
a pinch of salt
75 g (3 oz) unsalted butter, diced
2 tbsp caster sugar
2 egg yolks

Preheat the oven to 200°C/400°F/Gas Mark 6. Make the pastry. Sift the flour and salt into a bowl and rub in the butter until the mixture resembles fine breadcrumbs. Stir in the sugar and then work in the egg yolks to form a soft dough. Shape into a ball, flatten slightly and wrap in cling film. Chill for 20 minutes.

Divide the pastry in half (wrap half in cling film and freeze for later use). Cut the remaining pastry in half and roll each piece out thinly on a lightly floured surface and use to line two 10 cm (4 in) tartlet tins. Prick the bases and chill for 10 minutes.

Line the cases with baking paper and baking beans and bake for 15 minutes. Remove paper and beans and bake for a further 8–10 minutes until the pastry is crisp and golden. Leave to cool.

Cut the passionfruit in half and scoop the seeds into a bowl. Put the sugar and water into a saucepan and heat gently to dissolve the sugar. Bring to the boil, add the passionfruit pulp and simmer for 4–5 minutes until syrupy. Leave to cool.

Whip the cream and lemon curd until thickened, spoon into the pastry cases and serve drizzled with the passionfruit syrup.

ROASTED APRICOTS WITH ROSEWATER CREAM

Serves: 2
Preparation time: 15 minutes
Cooking time: 25 minutes

Rosewater is a flavouring used in Middle Eastern and North African cooking. It is available from larger supermarkets or delis. It adds a wonderful exotic flavour to both sweet and savoury dishes.

5 large ripe apricots, halved and stoned
grated zest and juice of $1/2$ orange
2 tbsp caster sugar
40 g (1$1/2$ oz) unsalted butter
25 g (1 oz) fresh wholemeal breadcrumbs
a pinch of ground cardamom
2 tsp grated unwaxed lemon zest
1 tbsp shelled pistachio nuts, roughly chopped

Rosewater and honey cream:
100 ml (3$1/2$ fl oz) double cream
1 tsp clear honey
2 tsp rosewater

Preheat the oven to 200°C/400°F/Gas Mark 6. Place the apricots cut-side up in a small baking dish, add the orange juice and half the sugar and bake for 10 minutes.

Melt 25 g (1 oz) of the butter in a frying pan, add the breadcrumbs and fry gently, stirring until golden. Add the cardamom, remaining sugar, orange and lemon zest and pistachio nuts.

Remove the apricots from the oven, sprinkle over the breadcrumb mixture and dot with the remaining butter. Return to the oven for a further 10 minutes.

Whip the cream with the honey and rosewater until stiff, and serve with the apricots.

RASPBERRY AND CASSIS PASTRIES

Serves: 4
Preparation time: 10 minutes
Cooking time: 10 minutes, plus cooling

The quantity of pastry in this recipes makes enough for 4 servings but the cooked pastries freeze well to be used later.

1 sheet ready-rolled puff pastry
vegetable oil spray
1 tbsp icing sugar, plus extra for dusting
200 g (7 oz) fresh raspberries
1 tbsp crème de cassis
100 ml (3$\frac{1}{2}$ fl oz) double cream

Preheat the oven to 220°C/425°F/Gas Mark 7. Remove the pastry from the freezer and thaw for 5 minutes. Cut the pastry diagonally into quarters to form 4 triangles and then each of those in half diagonally to form 8 small triangles.

Transfer to a baking tray and spray lightly with the oil. Put half the icing sugar into a fine sieve and dust the triangles all over. Bake for 10 minutes until the pastry is puffed up and golden. Transfer to a wire rack to cool. Freeze half the triangles for later use.

Place half the raspberries in a food processor with the cassis and remaining icing sugar and process until smooth. Pass through a fine sieve and set aside. Whip the cream until stiff.

To assemble the pastries, split each triangle almost in half with a sharp knife and fill each one with a quarter of the cream and raspberries. Arrange two on each plate, drizzle with the raspberry and cassis sauce, and serve dusted with icing sugar.

STRAWBERRIES WITH CARAMEL CREAM

Serves: 2
Preparation time: 10 minutes

An amazingly simple yet delicious dessert – the combination of soured cream and soft brown sugar make an instant caramel sauce, providing the perfect dip for strawberries or other fruits.

>250 g (8 oz) strawberries
>75 g (3 oz) soured cream
>2 tbsp soft light brown sugar
>
>dessert biscuits, to serve

Wash the strawberries and place on a large plate. Beat the soured cream and sugar together until silky, and spoon into a bowl.

Serve the strawberries with the cream and dessert biscuits.

EGGS AND DAIRY

Your weekly shop will include eggs and dairy products from which, with the help of your store cupboard, you can make any of the dishes below. The main fresh ingredients are highlighted in the fridge. Any extra flavourings, seasonings and side dishes are listed below.

130 **CHEESY MUSTARD AND LEEK TOASTS**

131 **COURGETTE AND RICOTTA FRITTATA**

132 **MALAYSIAN OMELETTE**

134 **FRAZZLED EGGS WITH OYSTER SAUCE**

135 **SCRAMBLED EGGS WITH SMOKED SALMON**

136 **COCONUT EGGY BREAD WITH GRILLED PEACHES**

137 **ICE CREAM AND AMARETTI BISCUITS WITH CHOCOLATE SAUCE**

138 **SUMMER FRUIT BRÛLÉE**

140 **HONEY MOUSSE WITH MANGO**

141 **BAKED COFFEE AND CARDAMOM CUSTARD**

142 **INDIVIDUAL TIRAMISU**

SMOKED SALMON
FRESH MIXED HERBS
FRESH CHIVES
GARLIC
BEANSPROUTS
SLICED BREAD
BRIOCHE, PANETTONE OR SWEET BREAD
OYSTER SAUCE
SWEET CHILLI SAUCE
THAI FISH SAUCE
WORCESTERSHIRE SAUCE
WHOLEGRAIN MUSTARD
CLEAR HONEY
COCONUT CREAM
DESICCATED COCONUT
GROUND CINNAMON
GROUND CARDAMOM
VANILLA ICE CREAM
AMARETTI BISCUITS
ALMOND THINS OR BISCOTTI
SAVOIR BISCUITS
ESPRESSO COFFEE
AMARETTO
LIGHT BEER

CHEESY MUSTARD AND LEEK TOASTS

Serves: 2
Preparation time: 5 minutes
Cooking time: 7–8 minutes

25 g (1 oz) butter
1 leek, finely sliced
75 g (3 oz) Grated gruyère or Cheddar cheese
1 egg yolk
2 tsp wholegrain mustard
a few drops Worcestershire sauce
2 tbsp light beer
salt and pepper
2 large slices bread

a green salad, to serve

Melt the butter in a saucepan and gently fry the leek for 5 minutes until softened. Transfer to a bowl and stir in the cheese, egg yolk, mustard, Worcestershire sauce, beer and salt and pepper.

Preheat the grill to high and toast the bread on both sides. Spoon over the leek mixture, spreading it almost to the edges of the bread. Grill the toasts for 2 minutes until the cheese is melted and golden, and just beginning to bubble. Serve hot with a green salad.

COURGETTE AND RICOTTA FRITTATA

Serves: 2
Preparation time: 10 minutes
Cooking time: 10 minutes

A frittata is an Italian omelette and differs from the more classic egg dish in that it is cooked completely in the pan, firstly on the stove and then under the grill.

> 1 large courgette (about 150 g/5 oz)
> 2 tbsp extra virgin olive oil
> 1 garlic clove, crushed
> 2 tsp chopped fresh tarragon
> salt and pepper
> 4 eggs
> 125 g (4 oz) ricotta
>
> freshly grated Parmesan, to serve

Cut the courgette into 5 mm/¼ in thick slices. Heat 1 tablespoon of the oil in a 23cm/9 in frying pan and stir-fry the courgettes and garlic over a medium heat for 2–3 minutes until lightly golden. Add the tarragon and a little seasoning.

Beat the eggs lightly with a balloon whisk and stir in the courgette mixture. Wipe the frying pan clean.

Preheat the grill to high. Heat the remaining oil in the clean pan and then pour in the egg mixture. Crumble over the ricotta and cook over a medium heat for 5 minutes until the egg is almost set. Transfer the pan to the grill and heat for a final 2–3 minutes to cook the top of the frittata. Sprinkle over the Parmesan and serve hot.

MALAYSIAN OMELETTE

Serves: 2
Preparation time: 5 minutes
Cooking time: 3 minutes

It is best to eat omelettes as soon as they are cooked so make the first one, serve and then make the second.

4 spring onions, finely chopped
2 large red chillies, deseeded and chopped
4 tbsp chopped fresh coriander
6 eggs, beaten
1 tbsp Thai fish sauce
1 tbsp water
a pinch Chinese five-spice powder

vegetable oil, for frying

To serve:
bean sprouts
fresh coriander leaves
sweet chilli sauce

Beat together the spring onions, chillies, coriander, eggs, fish sauce, water and Chinese five-spice powder until blended

Heat a little oil in a frying pan, add half the omelette mixture and cook, stirring a few times, for about 3 minutes until the mixture is almost set. Carefully slip the omelette out and on to a plate, folding it over as you go.

Repeat with the remaining mixture and serve the omelettes with bean sprouts, extra coriander and sweet chilli sauce.

FRAZZLED EGGS WITH OYSTER SAUCE

Serves: 2
Preparation time: 5 minutes
Cooking time: 5 minutes

In this recipe, the eggs are fried in really hot oil so that they are golden and crispy around the edges, giving a wonderful texture to the dish. They can be served as a brunch dish with toast or as part of an Asian meal.

1 tbsp sunflower oil, plus extra for shallow frying
1 garlic clove, sliced
2 tbsp oyster sauce
1 tbsp water
2 tsp light soy sauce
1 tsp caster sugar
2 large free-range eggs
1 spring onion, thinly sliced
1 small red chilli, deseeded and sliced

plain boiled rice, to serve (optional)

Heat the oil in a small saucepan and gently fry the garlic for 30 seconds until lightly golden. Add the oyster sauce, water, soy sauce and sugar and stir over a gentle heat until the sugar dissolves. Set aside.

Heat a shallow layer of oil in a non-stick frying pan and when it is really hot and starts smoking, fry the eggs for about 2 minutes until crispy around the edges and cooked to your liking.

Remove the eggs with a fish slice, shaking off excess oil, and serve drizzled with the oyster sauce mixture, topped with spring onions and chilli.

SCRAMBLED EGGS WITH SMOKED SALMON

Serves: 2
Preparation time: 5 minutes
Cooking time: 3 minutes

This makes a perfect brunch dish for a special occasion.

6 eggs
50 ml (2 fl oz) cream
1 tbsp chopped fresh chives
salt and pepper
25 g (1 oz) butter
125 g (4 oz) smoked salmon, cut into strips

buttered toast, to serve

Crack the eggs into a bowl and whisk in the cream, chives and a little salt and pepper. Melt the butter in a non-stick saucepan, add the egg mixture and stir over a low heat for 2–3 minutes until just beginning to set.

Stir in the smoked salmon, cook for a final 30 seconds or so and spoon on to buttered toast. Serve hot.

COCONUT EGGY BREAD WITH GRILLED PEACHES

Serves: 2
Preparation time: 5 minutes
Cooking time: 7 minutes

Brioche loaves are available from some larger supermarkets but any sweet bread can be used for this recipe.

2 large ripe peaches, halved and stoned
1½ tsp clear honey
a pinch of ground cinnamon
75 ml (3 fl oz) coconut cream
1 egg, lightly beaten
1 tbsp caster sugar
25 g (1 oz) unsalted butter
2 large slices brioche, panettone or other sweet bread

To serve:
whipped cream
toasted desiccated coconut

Preheat the grill. Place the peaches cut-side up on the grill pan. Combine the honey and cinnamon, drizzle over the peaches and grill for 5 minutes until blistered and softened.

Beat the coconut cream, egg and sugar together in a bowl. Melt the butter in a frying pan, dip the bread into the coconut mixture and then fry in the butter for 1 minute each side until golden.

Transfer the bread to warmed plates, top with the grilled peaches and serve with whipped cream and toasted coconut.

ICE CREAM AND AMARETTI BISCUITS WITH CHOCOLATE SAUCE

Serves: 2
Preparation time: 5 minutes
Cooking time: 2–3 minutes

This quick dessert is half-way between an ice cream sundae and a trifle. Use whatever flavour ice cream you want.

> 100 g (3^1/$_2$ oz) plain chocolate, chopped
> 55g (2^1/$_2$ oz) unsalted butter, diced
> 4 small scoops vanilla ice cream
> 50 g (2 oz) amaretti biscuits, crushed

   Place the chocolate and butter in a bowl and set over a saucepan of gently simmering water (do not allow the base of the bowl to touch the water). Stir until the chocolate has melted and the mixture is smooth. Remove from the heat and leave to cool.

   Spoon the ice cream and crushed amaretti biscuits into glasses and pour over the chocolate sauce. Serve at once.

SUMMER FRUIT BRÛLÉE

Serves: 2
Preparation time: 10 minutes
Cooking time: 2–3 minutes

The fruits should be just warm underneath their blanket of sugar crusted cream.

> 125 g (4 oz) mascarpone cheese
> 125 g (4 oz) Greek yogurt
> 250 g (8 oz) prepared mixed summer fruits, such as peaches,
>   strawberries, raspberries and blueberries
> 2 tbsp demerara sugar

Preheat the grill to high. Beat the mascarpone and yogurt together until smooth. Arrange the fruits in 2 small gratin dishes and spread the mascarpone mixture over the fruits.

Sprinkle the demerara sugar over the top and grill for 3–4 minutes until the sugar is melted and bubbling. Serve at once.

HONEY MOUSSE WITH MANGO

Serves: 2
Preparation time: 10 minutes
Chilling time: 30 minutes

1 egg, separated
175 g (6 oz) Greek yogurt
2 tbsp clear honey
75 ml (3 fl oz) whipping cream
1 large mango, peeled, stoned and diced

almond thins or biscotti, to serve

Beat the egg yolk, yogurt and honey together in a bowl. Whip the cream until it holds its shape and fold into the yogurt mixture. Wash the whisk or beaters, dry thoroughly and whisk the egg white until stiff. Carefully fold into the yogurt mixture.

Divide the mango and the mousse mixture in 2 glasses layering them and finishing with the mango. Chill for 30 minutes before serving.

BAKED COFFEE AND CARDAMOM CUSTARD

Serves: 2
Preparation time: 5 minutes
Cooking time: 30 minutes

150 ml (¼ pint) milk
150 ml (¼ pint) double cream
½ tsp ground cardamom
1 egg
1 egg yolk
50 g (2 oz) caster sugar
50 ml (2 fl oz) freshly made espresso coffee

Preheat the oven to 150°C/300°F/Gas Mark 2. Place the milk, cream and cardamom in a saucepan and heat gently until the mixture reaches boiling point. Beat the egg, egg yolk, sugar and coffee together and stir in the heated milk mixture until smooth.

Strain the mixture into two 200 ml (7 fl oz) ramekin dishes and place in a roasting tin. Half fill the tin with boiling water and bake the custards for 30 minutes until set. Remove from the oven and leave to cool. Serve warm or cold.

INDIVIDUAL TIRAMISU

Serves: 2
Preparation time: 5 minutes, plus soaking
Chilling time: 30 minutes

Amaretto is an almond-flavoured liqueur available from most good supermarkets or wine shops. It adds a lovely nutty flavour to this Italian trifle.

> 2 savoir biscuits
> 4 tbsp espresso coffee (left to go cold)
> 3 tbsp Amaretto
> 40 g (1$^{1}/_{2}$ oz) coarsely grated dark chocolate
> 125 g (4 oz) mascarpone cheese
> 75 ml (3 fl oz) double cream
> 2 tbsp icing sugar
> 2 egg whites

Break the biscuits in half and divide between 2 large glasses. Combine the coffee and 2 tablespoons of Amaretto and pour over the biscuits. Leave to soak for 15 minutes and then scatter over half the chocolate.

Beat the mascarpone, cream, sugar and remaining Amaretto together. Whisk the egg whites in a separate bowl and fold into the mascarpone mixture. Spoon over the biscuits, top with the remaining chocolate and chill for 30 minutes.

COOL SHARING

RAID THE FRIDGE FOR RECIPES— FEEDING FRIENDS

Louise Pickford

Now that you have fallen in love with your fridge for everyday eating, you might like to share your culinary skills with friends and family. Cool Sharing by Louise Pickford takes cool inspiration to the next level for easy entertaining.